3~

Understanding

The Lord of
the Rings

Understanding

The Lord of
the Rings

New and future titles in the Understanding Great Literature series include:

Understanding

The Lord of the Rings

UNDERSTANDING GREAT LITERATURE

Ted Hodges

LUCENT
BOOKS ®

THOMSON
——✷——™
GALE

San Diego • Detroit • New York • San Francisco • Cleveland
New Haven, Conn. • Waterville, Maine • London • Munich

© 2003 by Lucent Books. Lucent Books is an imprint of The Gale Group, Inc.,
a division of Thomson Learning, Inc.

Lucent Books® and Thomson Learning™ are trademarks used herein under license.

For more information, contact
Lucent Books
27500 Drake Rd.
Farmington Hills, MI 48331-3535
Or you can visit our Internet site at http://www.gale.com

LIBRARY OF CONGRESS CATALOGING-IN-PUBLICATION DATA

Hodges, Ted, 1947–
   Understanding the lord of the rings / by Ted Hodges.
      v. cm. — (Understanding great literature)
   Includes bibliographical references and index.
   Contents: The author of the century—J.R.R. Tolkien's life and works—Influences and
sources of the Ring trilogy—The major characters and races—Major themes
explored in the trilogy.
   ISBN 1-59018-234-0 (hardback : alk. paper)
      1. Tolkien, J. R. R. (John Ronald Reuel), 1892–1973. Lord of the rings—Juvenile
literature. 2. Fantasy fiction, English—History and criticism—Juvenile literature.
3. Middle Earth (Imaginary place)—Juvenile literature. [1. Tolkien, J. R. R. (John
Ronald Reuel), 1892–1973. Lord of the rings. 2. English literature—History and
criticism.] I. Title. II. Series.
   PR6039.O32 L6363 2003
   823'.912—dc21
                                                                        2002013087

Printed in the United States of America

Contents

FOREWORD

"**E**xcept for a living man, there is nothing more wonderful than a book!" wrote the widely respected nineteenth-century teacher and writer Charles Kingsley. A book, he continued, "is a message to us from human souls we never saw. And yet these [books] arouse us, terrify us, teach us, comfort us, open our hearts to us as brothers." There are many different kinds of books, of course; and Kingsley was referring mainly to those containing literature—novels, plays, short stories, poems, and so on. In particular, he had in mind those works of literature that were and remain widely popular with readers of all ages and from many walks of life.

Such popularity might be based on one or several factors. On the one hand, a book might be read and studied by people in generation after generation because it is a literary classic, with characters and themes of universal relevance and appeal. Homer's epic poems, the *Iliad* and the *Odyssey*, Chaucer's *Canterbury Tales*, Shakespeare's *Hamlet* and *Romeo and Juliet*, and Dickens's *A Christmas Carol* fall into this category. Some popular books, on the other hand, are more controversial. Mark Twain's *Huckleberry Finn* and J.D. Salinger's *The Catcher in the Rye*, for instance, have their legions of devoted fans who see them as great literature; while others view them as less than worthy because of their racial depictions, profanity, or other factors.

Still another category of popular literature includes realistic modern fiction, including novels such as Robert Cormier's *I Am the Cheese* and S.E. Hinton's *The Outsiders*. Their keen social insights and sharp character portrayals have consistently reached out to and captured the imaginations of many teenagers and young adults; and for this reason they are often assigned and studied in schools.

These and other similar works have become the "old standards" of the literary scene. They are the ones that people most often read, discuss, and study; and each has, by virtue of its content, critical success, or just plain longevity, earned the right to be the subject of a book examining its content. (Some, of course, like the *Iliad* and *Hamlet*, have been the subjects of numerous books already; but their literary stature is so lofty that there can never be too many books about them!) For millions of readers and students in one generation after another, each of these works becomes, in a sense, an adventure in appreciation, enjoyment, and learning.

The main purpose of Lucent's Understanding Great Literature series is to aid the reader in that ongoing literary adventure. Each volume in the series focuses on a single literary work that a majority of critics and teachers view as a classic and/or that is widely studied and discussed in schools. A typical volume first tells why the work in question is important. Then follow detailed overviews of the author's life, the work's historical background, its plot, its characters, and its themes. Numerous quotes from the work, as well as by critics and other experts, are interspersed throughout and carefully documented with footnotes for those who wish to pursue further research. Also included is a list of ideas for essays and other student projects relating to the work, an appendix of literary criticisms and analyses by noted scholars, and a comprehensive annotated bibliography.

The great nineteenth-century American poet Henry David Thoreau once quipped: "Read the best books first, or you may not have a chance to read them at all." For those who are reading or about to read the "best books" in the literary canon, the comprehensive, thorough, and thoughtful volumes of the Understanding Great Literature series are indispensable guides and sources of enrichment.

The Author of the Century

In the mid-1990s, the English-speaking literary world experienced a quite unexpected and extraordinary revelation. When a major British newspaper polled twenty-five thousand readers, asking them to name their picks for the greatest books of the twentieth century, J.R.R. Tolkien's *The Lord of the Rings* was rated number one. Many self-styled "serious" literary critics were dumbfounded. To them, Tolkien's three-volume work of fantasy-adventure, often called the "Ring trilogy" for short, was nothing more than a highly overrated children's story. They remembered and agreed with some of the negative reviews that had accompanied the trilogy's release in the mid-1950s. Noted critic Edmund Wilson had called it "an overgrown fairy story," "long winded," and "fantasy for its own sake." "Dr. Tolkien has little skill at narrative," Wilson wrote, "and no instinct for literary form."[1] Later, another critic called the trilogy "inflated, overwritten . . . and moralistic in the extreme."[2]

Believing that Tolkien's placing first in the poll was some kind of fluke or accident, such critics called for other polls. Several newspapers and national book dealers obliged, among them Waterstone's Bookstore, which conducted a poll of twenty-six thousand readers in 1996. Again, *The Lord of the Rings* scored first place, as it did in a similar poll sponsored by Britain's prestigious Folio Society.

Clearly, the popularity of Tolkien's Ring trilogy is no fluke. Nor is it confined to Britain, the United States, and other English-speaking lands. More than 100 million copies of Tolkien's books have been sold worldwide and the trilogy has been translated into twenty-five languages. In addition, what might be termed Tolkien "mania" has spawned both animated and live-action movies; countless copycat novels constituting a massive and lucrative fantasy-fiction literary market; role-playing games such as *Dungeons and Dragons;* sword and sorcery video games; calendar art and musical renditions; and thousands of Internet websites. In addition, Tolkien's books have inspired millions of young people in several generations to read more than just comic books and obligatory school assignments.

Dressed as characters of Middle-earth, these fans of The Lord of the Rings *are just a few of Tolkien's many admirers from around the world.*

Grandeur and Terror

The question naturally raised by this remarkable track record is "Why?" How can the tremendous size of the trilogy's loyal audience, as well as its continued and unwavering endurance, be explained? The answer to this question is manifold. First, if nothing else, the work is great escapist fare. Tolkien leads the reader into another world, a place of wonder, magic, and adventure, allowing him or her temporarily to set aside the mundane worries of the real world. The key to his success in this respect is the extraordinary detail and air of believability Tolkien creates in that other world. As the great English poet W.H. Auden put it:

> No previous writer has, to my knowledge, created an imaginary world and a feigned history in such detail. By the time the reader has finished the trilogy . . . he knows as much about Mr. Tolkien's Middle-earth, its landscape, its fauna and flora, its peoples, their languages, their history, their cultural habits, as . . . he knows about the actual world. Mr. Tolkien's world may not be the same as our own . . . but it is a world of intelligible law, not mere wish; the reader's sense of the credible is never violated.[3]

Another virtue of the Ring trilogy is that it is told on a grand scale and deals with larger-than-life characters, events, and ideas. On first reading it, Tolkien's colleague, the great English writer C.S. Lewis, remarked: "Once it gets underway, the steady upward slope of grandeur and terror . . . is almost unequalled in the whole range of narrative art known to me."[4] Themes and events such as world war, entire races threatened with genocide, the forces of good battling the forces of evil, the human struggle against corruption, and the nature of heroism are painted on the enormous canvas normally reserved for the exploits of heroic mythology. Indeed, the story told in the trilogy was inspired by and is in some ways a new version of some of Western civilization's major ancient and medieval myths. This gives the work a strong cultural foundation in the real world, a base on which the author constructs his phenomenally detailed alternate world.

The Ring trilogy also appeals to many readers because it taps into their worries and fears about the real world in their own time. The story tells of a pleasant, almost idyllic preindustrial society that is threatened by the forces of greed, corruption, evil, and autocratic power. And large numbers of readers have detected in it a parallel with many destructive events of the twentieth century. Tolkien "seems on the face of it to be an antiquarian author writing about an imaginary far past," points out T.A. Shippey, author of *J.R.R. Tolkien: Author of the Century.* However,

> I am convinced that the reason he consistently wins the polls [for best book of the century] is that his work articulates [puts into words] some of the deepest and most specific concerns of the twentieth century—concerns such as industrialized warfare, the temptations of power, the origins of evil, [and] the failure of good intentions and righteous causes. . . . He answers questions that have deeply preoccupied ordinary people, but that have not been answered by the official . . . speakers of our culture—writers, politicians, philosophers. The most obvious one is, Why has the twentieth century been so unremittingly evil? [5]

The Strengths Outweigh the Shortcomings

Tolkien never asks this question directly in the trilogy, of course. Personally, he was not concerned with political commentary, and most of what his legions of fans have read into the work may not have been consciously intended on his part. He was much more concerned with telling a good story that would entertain people. "I hope that those who have read *The Lord of the Rings* with pleasure," he wrote in 1964, "will not think me ungrateful. To please readers was my main object, and to be assured of this [by the book's widespread popularity] has been a great reward." [6]

13

For Tolkien, this reward easily outweighed the stings and barbs of the few who did not like the work and who were perplexed by its high place in the polls. At the same time, he was gracious and modest in the face of such criticism, even when it was harsh and mean-spirited. "Some of those who have read the book," he said,

> have found it boring, absurd, or contemptible; and I have no cause to complain. . . . It is perhaps not possible in a long tale to please everybody at all points. . . . The most critical reader of all, myself, now finds many defects, minor and major, but being fortunately under no obligation either to review the book or to write it again, he will pass over these in silence.[7]

These words show that Tolkien was not hesitant to admit his work was flawed. And certainly some of the critiques leveled at his literary abilities have credibility and merit. Yet as repeated

Tolkien relaxes in his study. A philologist (expert on languages) by trade, he was intimately familiar with Old English, Anglo-Saxon, and other dead tongues and their literatures.

polls have shown, over the years tens of millions of readers have agreed that any shortcomings to be found in the Ring trilogy are rendered insignificant by its many strengths. Perhaps no one has phrased it better than critic Scott Rosenberg. The three books "are surely not perfect," he says.

> [They] contain little humor, pitifully few female characters, and even less in the way of romance with a small "r." But as a vast vision of the absolute corruption of absolute power—and the depths of courage that ordinary people . . . can find to oppose it—Tolkien's work remains incomparable.[8]

CHAPTER ONE

J.R.R. Tolkien's Life and Works

Though John Ronald Reuel Tolkien was born on January 3, 1892, in Bloemfontein, a town in central South Africa, he remained English to the core throughout his life. His father, Arthur Tolkien, and mother, Mabel Suffield Tolkien, had originally lived in Birmingham, in northeastern Warwickshire, England. But in 1890, Arthur, a banker, received an offer to take a rewarding position in a bank in Bloemfontein. He accepted and, at age thirty-five, he moved to South Africa alone; Mabel, fifteen years his junior, followed a year later. They were married in Cape Town on April 16, 1891, and were soon blessed with two fine sons—J.R.R., whom family and friends called Ronald, and his only sibling, Hilary, born in February 1894.

The Tolkiens were not destined to make a permanent home together in Bloemfontein, however. South Africa's climate and lifestyle did not appeal to Mabel, and she was homesick for her friends and family back in England. Also, the excessive heat of the country bothered young Ronald, who began to experience bouts of sickness.

Return to England

So in November 1894, Mabel Tolkien decided to book passage back to England for herself and two sons, hoping that an extended holiday there would be good for both her and Ronald. Arthur Tolkien wanted to join his family, but his workload at the bank was too great. Mabel and the boys left South Africa in April 1895 and arrived in England three weeks later. They moved in with Mabel's parents in their small house on the outskirts of Birmingham, and Ronald's health immediately began to improve. He later recalled:

> My earliest memories are of Africa, but it was alien to me, and when I came home, therefore, I had for the countryside of England both the native feeling and the personal wonder of somebody who comes to it. I came to the English countryside when I was about $3\frac{1}{2}$ or 4—it seemed to me wonderful.[9]

Meanwhile, back in South Africa, Arthur Tolkien's health quickly declined. In November 1895 he contracted rheumatic

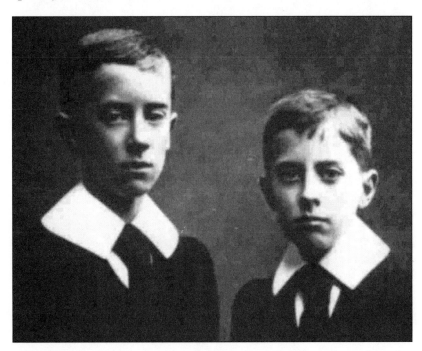

J.R.R. Tolkien (left) poses with his younger brother, Hilary, for a photo taken around the turn of the last century.

fever. And on February 15, 1896, he died suddenly of a brain hemorrhage. This left Mabel, at age twenty-six, the sole parent of two young children. She had an income from some investments her husband had made, but it was small and hardly enough to support a family. For the moment she accepted some

Tolkien spent several of his earliest years in this cottage near Birmingham, England.

modest financial help from relatives, hoping to supplement it by tutoring or otherwise putting to good use her ability to read and write Latin, French, and German.

In the years immediately following her husband's death, Mabel Tolkien made some choices for her sons that would end up affecting their lives profoundly. First, she converted the family from Protestantism to Catholicism. This caused bad feelings among both relatives and friends because anti-Catholic prejudice was widespread at that time. And those family members who had been giving Mabel financial aid cut her off. Luckily for young Ronald and his brother, a kindly Catholic priest, Father Francis Xavier Morgan, befriended the Tolkiens. He became a father figure for the boys and eventually their legal guardian.

Mabel also moved her family to a small rented cottage in the hamlet of Sarehole, a couple of miles south of Birmingham. The lovely rural setting had a strong effect on J.R.R. Tolkien, instilling in him a deep love for nature and stimulating his already fertile imagination. "The village and its nearby mill embodied the core of the glorious English countryside," one of his biographers writes.

> Browns and greens and yellows washing together in a sea of delight. The sun dancing timeless jigs on the cornfields and the ancient barn roofs. Hills and vales, adventure and games. . . . There were the local characters, eccentric but harmless, and all, in one shape or another, would find their way into Tolkien's later writings. At the nearby mill, for instance, the old man with the long, dark beard frightened the lives out of the boys. Worse was his son, who would rush out of the same mill covered in flour, white from head to toe. As he chased the boys away he shouted and screamed. They called him the White Ogre. Another local was called the Black Ogre, after he pursued Tolkien after the little lad had trespassed. [10]

An Affinity for Languages

In addition, Mabel began educating her sons at home. She passed along her considerable knowledge of drawing, painting, and playing the piano. And she taught them Latin, French, and German, which initiated Tolkien's lifelong love of words and languages. Mabel provided the boys with books, as well. Tolkien became especially enchanted with legends, adventure, and fantasy; some of his favorites were *Alice in Wonderland*, *The Red Indian Stories*, and the "Curdie" books of George MacDonald, written in a heavy Scottish dialect for both children and adults. Tolkien was especially fond of Andrew Lang's *Red Fairy Book*, which contained the story of the Norse hero Sigurd, who slew the fierce dragon Fafnir. "I desired dragons with a profound desire," Tolkien remembered later. "Of course, I in my timid body did not wish to have them in the neighborhood. But the world that contained even the imagination of Fafnir was richer and more beautiful, at whatever cost of peril." [11]

The attention Mabel Tolkien devoted to teaching her sons stemmed from her strong belief in the importance of a good education. In 1899, she felt her eldest son was ready for more formal schooling and had him take the entrance exam to King Edward's School in Birmingham, which his father had attended. He failed. But the following year he passed and began making the daily four-mile trek to school from the house in Sarehole. Worried that the long walk would overtax the boy, Mabel moved the family closer to the city.

Young J.R.R. Tolkien prospered at school. In particular, he showed an astounding ability to learn entire languages in very short time spans. In only a few months he mastered Greek; and as a member of the school's debating society he took on the role of a Greek ambassador who spoke entirely in Greek. He also learned Old English. Another time, he astonished his classmates by speaking in fluent Gothic, an ancient northern European tongue; and later, he made another stir when he spoke in Anglo-Saxon, a language used in early medieval England.

Tolkien's affinity for languages and exploration of words and their roots laid the foundation for his later career as a philologist (an expert on languages, especially as used in literature). These abilities also inspired him to begin inventing his own languages. He called his first experiment "Nevbosh," meaning New Nonsense. The phrase *Dar fys ma vel gom co palt 'Hoc Pys go iskeli far maino woc?'*, for instance, translated as "There was an old man who said 'How can I possibly carry my cow?'" Looking back as an adult, Tolkien maintained:

> It's not that uncommon, you know. An enormously greater number of children have what you might call a creative element in them than is usually supposed, and it isn't necessarily limited to certain things. They may not want to paint or draw, or have much music, but they nevertheless want to create something. And if the main mass of education takes a linguistic form, their creation will take a linguistic form. It's so extraordinarily common, I once did think that their ought to be some organized research into it.[12]

In November 1904, young Ronald Tolkien's school activities were temporarily interrupted when his mother, who had been ill for several months, fell into a diabetic coma and died. Her passing had a profound effect on the young man. He recognized how hard she had worked to support him and Hilary after they had been scorned for converting to Catholicism. "My own dear mother was a martyr indeed," he wrote nine years later, "and it is not to everybody that God grants so easy a

Tolkien as he appeared in his freshman year at Oxford.

way to his great gifts as he did to Hilary and myself, giving us a mother who killed herself with labor and trouble to ensure us keeping the faith." [13]

On to Oxford

After his mother's death, Tolkien's personality steadily changed. He was once carefree and looked at the future as full of promise. Now he increasingly felt unsure and pessimistic about life and where it might lead him. Thereafter he periodically suffered from bouts of despair, becoming convinced that all might be lost or that the battle of life could never be won. These fears would later be reflected in some of the themes and situations in his masterpiece, *The Lord of the Rings*.

Whatever negative feelings the young man had, all was clearly not lost for him in the months and years following his mother's passing. Father Morgan became the boys' guardian, as Mabel Tolkien had wanted, and fulfilled that role admirably. Morgan saw to it that they were housed and fed in a private home. There, at

Some of the picturesque buildings and grounds of Exeter College, at Oxford. Tolkien studied there from 1911 to 1915.

age sixteen, Tolkien met Edith Bratt, then nineteen, another orphan, and the two fell in love. But because both were still very young, marriage was out of the question. Undaunted, they vowed to remain true to each other and wait at least until Edith was twenty-one.

In the meantime, Father Morgan also made sure that Tolkien and his brother remained in school. J.R.R. Tolkien continued to excel in his studies at King Edward's School, and in 1910 was accepted to the prestigious Oxford University. At Oxford, Tolkien started out majoring in the classics; but his heart was not in the work, and after two years he switched to the English department so that he could focus all of his energies on the study of languages, his first love.

While at Oxford, Tolkien also became friends with Joseph Wright, a respected philology professor. A brilliant individual, Wright was an expert in ancient languages, including Sanskrit, Gothic, Old Bulgarian, Lithuanian, Russian, Old Norse, Old German, and Old English. His influence on Tolkien was nothing less than immense. Tolkien later remembered "the vastness of Joe Wright's dining-room table, when I sat alone at one end learning the elements of Greek philology from the glinting glasses in the further gloom."[14] When Wright discovered that the young language enthusiast was interested in learning Welsh, a language with Celtic roots, he advised, "Go in for Celtic, lad. There's money in [teaching and writing about] it."[15]

At about this time, Tolkien also discovered a text on Finnish grammar, and with its help he returned to the *Kalevala,* the Finnish heroic epic, which he had earlier read. Fascinated by medieval European myths, he had thoroughly enjoyed the English translations of the poems and stories contained in this work. But he had no idea what they sounded like in the original Finnish. As he dove into learning Finnish, he was excited at being able to read passages of the ancient work without the need of translation. Later he said that "it was like discovering a wine-cellar filled with bottles of amazing wine of a kind and flavor never tasted before."[16] Tolkien also explained what he saw as the literary importance of these old Finnish poems, saying that they represented the survival of a pure, ancient European literary tradition. That tradition had been largely lost or watered down over the centuries. "These mythological ballads," he stated,

> are full of that primitive undergrowth that the literature of Europe has on the whole been steadily cutting and reducing for many centuries with different and earlier completeness among different people. . . . I would that we had more of it left—something of the same sort that belonged to the English.[17]

Tolkien's mastery of Finnish would eventually inspire his invention of a private language—Quenya or High Elven—which would become an integral feature of the great Ring trilogy.

Not all of Tolkien's time at Oxford was taken up by his rigorous studies. Though bookish and introverted in some ways, he was also a friendly and social individual who enjoyed the company of his fellow students. He became a member of the Essay Club, took part in the Debating Society, and played rugby. He also smoked a pipe and enjoyed late nights of literary and political talk and debate with his male friends. Indeed, throughout the rest of his life, Tolkien made a clear distinction between his home life, eventually including a wife and children, and that of his male companions. This preference for male companionship and his acceptance of the prevailing male-dominated society are also reflected in *The Lord of the Rings*. Many critics have taken the books of the trilogy to task for their general lack of strong female characters. The truth is that, despite his great intellect and civilized manners, Tolkien, like most men of his generation, was a creature of his upbringing and remained content with the social status quo.

Tolkien the Soldier

The next major phase in Tolkien's life began in 1914, when England declared war on Germany and World War I erupted in

Europe. Tolkien wanted to enlist and fight for his country. But he also desired to finish his degree at the university before enlisting. So he joined Britain's Officer's Training Corps, a military organization that would allow him to continue his studies while training. His final exams resulted in first-class honors. He was overjoyed, knowing that this distinction would later open many doors and almost certainly help him find a prestigious academic position. For the moment, however, it was time for Tolkien to fulfill his military obligations.

Before leaving for the European battlefront, Tolkien finally married his childhood sweetheart, Edith Bratt. The ceremony took place on March 22, 1916. This new stage of their lives had barely begun when Tolkien received his embarkation orders. On June 4, 1916, he left England for Calais, France.

Tolkien as a soldier in World War I (left); and his childhood sweetheart, Edith Bratt. They were married shortly before he shipped out for France.

While in France, Tolkien grew close to and gained respect for his fellow soldiers, especially the NCOs (noncommissioned officers), writing later that "My Sam Gamgee [one of the hobbits in *The Lord of the Rings*] is indeed a reflection of the English soldier, of the privates . . . I knew in the 1914 war, and recognized as so far superior to myself."[18]

In July 1916, Tolkien's unit was ordered to the front. And there he experienced some of the terrible things that only those who have been in combat can truly describe—dead men, broken bodies, the smell of rotting flesh, the despair of minds torn and twisted from the ravages of war, and whole landscapes blasted and stripped of their green. Tolkien himself became a casualty of these horrors when he was struck down by "trench fever," an ailment characterized by a prolonged high body temperature. He ended up in the army hospital but eventually had to be sent back to England to recover. In this way, his personal experience with the terrors of war ended; however, the indelible images of what he had witnessed would remain with him and inevitably find their way into his writings.

Early Academic Jobs and Writings

Now that he was home and reunited with Edith, Tolkien began to work in earnest on his own version of the European heroic legends he found so fascinating. The idea had been growing within him for a long time to create an ancient mythology for England, and now that idea started to take shape. On the cover of a notebook he wrote "The Book of Lost Tales," which would eventually become a huge epic, *The Silmarillion*. The first parts of this work, the story of which takes place *before* the one told in *The Lord of the Rings*, describe the creation of the universe and the earthlike realm he called Middle-earth. At the time, Tolkien could not foresee that he would work on *The Silmarillion* at intervals for the rest of his life and end up dying before it was finished.

In 1920, while working on his new mythology, Tolkien landed his first academic position, becoming a reader (teaching

Tolkien, Edith, and their children enjoy some leisure time at their home at 22 Northmoon Road, in Oxford, where they lived from 1925 to 1930.

assistant) in English languages at the University of Leeds, in north-central England. Two years later, he published his first major literary work, *A Middle English Vocabulary,* a glossary of medieval English terms. Also while at Leeds, Tolkien edited the medieval adventure story in verse form, *Sir Gawain and the Green Knight.* His edition of this work is still the most widely used by students in the English-speaking world.

Tolkien made such a name for himself at Leeds that other schools took notice. In 1925 he accepted the job of Rawlinson and Bosworth Professor of Anglo-Saxon at Pembroke College at Oxford. There, over the next two decades, he completed several important works. Many of these were of a scholarly nature and are often overlooked in the glare of his widely popular fiction. Two of the more important early scholarly works he produced at Oxford were *Chaucer as a Philologist* (1934) and *Beowulf: The Monster and the Critics* (1936).

Making these early academic years extra busy for Tolkien was the job of helping Edith raise a family. By the time he started teaching at Oxford, they already had three small children—John Francis (born in 1917), Michael Hilary (1920), and Christopher Reuel (1924). A daughter, Priscilla, came along in 1929. Tolkien thoroughly loved his children and proved to be an attentive father. "Children liberated him," biographer Michael Coren writes, and "provided him with a new vision of the world. The ordinary became the extraordinary through the eyes of a child. It was a view Tolkien relished."[19]

"There Lived a Hobbit"

In fact, it is possible that if Tolkien had never had any children, his books about hobbits may never have been written. Like countless parents before and after him, he enjoyed telling bedtime stories to his children. One of these stories was of his own invention—a formative version of what would later become *The Hobbit*. The basic idea had come to him a few years before in a rather casual way. He later recalled that he was correcting exams and

Tolkien's literary colleague and friend C.S. Lewis in a photo taken in 1950.

one of the candidates had mercifully left one of the pages with no writing on it (which is the best thing that can happen to an examiner) and I wrote on it: "In a hole in the ground there lived a hobbit." Names always generate a story in my mind. Eventually I thought I'd better find out what hobbits were like. But that's only the beginning.[20]

From that beginning, the tale quickly developed, growing more complex and detailed in repeated tellings to the children. It took place in the land Tolkien had already chosen as the center of his new mythology—Middle-earth—and chronicled the adventures of an undersized hero who encounters nasty goblins and a dragon guarding a treasure.

One day a family friend mentioned to a representative of a respected publisher, Allen and Unwin, that Professor Tolkien had a children's story of unusual merit. Encouraged by his friend and fellow Oxford professor, C.S. Lewis (author of the popular *Chronicles of Narnia*), Tolkien submitted a written sketch of the tale to Stanley Unwin late in 1936. Unwin, who believed that the best judge of children's books are children themselves, handed the story to his ten-year-old son, Rayner, to read and review. The boy's initial report read:

> Bilbo Baggins was a hobbit who lived in his hobbit-hole and *never* went for adventures, [but] at last Gandalf the Wizard and his dwarves perswaded him to go. He had a very exiting time fighting goblins and wargs. At last they got to the lonely mountain; Smaug, the dragon who gawreds it is killed and after a terrific battle with the goblins he returned home-rich! This book, with the help of maps, does not need any illustrations; it is good and should appeal to all children between the ages of 5 and 9. [Misspellings in the original.][21]

For this review, Rayner was paid a shilling (equivalent to a few pennies). Unwin then gave the green light. Tolkien made some additions and revisions; and on September 21, 1937, *The Hobbit* was published.

In the eyes of history, Rayner Unwin must be credited with remarkable foresight. *The Hobbit* became an instant financial success as the first edition sold out before Christmas. It has since gone through numerous printings and sold more than 40 million copies, making it one of the most widely read children's books of all time. For the most part, it was also a critical success, both in England and the United States, with the *New York Herald Tribune,* among others, naming it the best children's book of the year.

Written in Blood

Thrilled by this success, Allen and Unwin naturally wanted Tolkien to write more about Middle-earth and its diverse peoples and creatures. So he began creating a sequel to *The Hobbit*. The new work turned out to be much grander in scale than the first one, however. It took him nearly fourteen years to finish; he worked on it at intervals and hardly at all during World War II (1939–1945). During that conflict, he filled most of what little spare time he had volunteering as an air raid warden and taking in needy lodgers who had been driven from their homes by German bombing.

Another reason the work took so long was that Tolkien was a stickler for detail and fussed over the manuscript, often revising or throwing out earlier material. Later he told Stanley Unwin: "It is written in my life-blood, such as that is, thick or thin."[22] As the work progressed, Tolkien read some of the story to the "Inklings," a group of fellow professors and professional men that also included C.S. Lewis, Warren Lewis (brother of C.S.), and R.E. Harvard. They met on Thursday nights at C.S. Lewis's house and took turns reading manuscripts, written by themselves or others, to the group. Reactions to Tolkien's new work were generally favorable, especially from C.S. Lewis, who said after reading the final draft: "The faults I think I can find could only delay and impair appreciation. The substantial splendor of the tale can carry them all. . . . I congratulate you. All the long years you have spent on it are justified."[23]

When Tolkien finally submitted the new work, titled *The Lord of the Rings*, to Allen and Unwin in the early 1950s, all involved agreed that it must be published. The problem was its inordinate length—more than half a million words, which the publisher feared might intimidate readers. Unwin suggested releasing it in three installments; at first, Tolkien objected, but he finally relented. The three volumes—*The Fellowship of the Ring, The Two Towers,* and *The Return of the King*—appeared in 1954–1955. The reviews were mixed. Nevertheless, a number of critics saw the work's merits from the start, foreshadowing the way future generations would see it. The London *Sunday Telegraph* placed it "among the greatest works of imaginary fiction of the twentieth century,"[24] and the *New York Times* declared that "the story moves on with a tremendous narrative rush to its climax. . . . [It is] an extraordinarily imaginative work, part saga, part allegory, and wholly exciting."[25]

Having published the Ring trilogy, Tolkien devoted the rest of his years to teaching and to attempting to finish *The Silmarillion*. From 1945 until his retirement in 1959, he taught English at Merton College at Oxford. There, both students and fans eagerly sought him out, as did television companies wanting to interview him. He sometimes found all this attention annoying, but overall he was grateful for the adulation and received it in a friendly manner. As for *The Silmarillion*, Tolkien's busy schedule, advancing age, and the sheer size and complexity of the story slowed the writing, and he finally gave up on it. His youngest son, Christopher, agreed to finish it for him and it was finally published in 1977.

J.R.R. and Edith Tolkien enjoyed his retirement years, although their time together turned out to be shorter than they had

Tolkien and Edith pose together shortly before her death in 1971. Tolkien himself passed away in 1973, saddening millions of people.

hoped. She died in 1971. And he followed her on September 2, 1973, at the age of eighty-one. (The immediate cause of death was listed as an infection in the chest.) As millions of people around the world mourned, the *Daily Telegraph* reassured them with a memorial that aptly summed up Tolkien's singular contribution. It read in part:

> His creatures were so real . . . that the Merton Professor of the English Language has acquired, like them, a certain timelessness. He was Gandalf the ageless Wizard, appearing and shaping the destiny of vast upland kingdoms, full of imagery and the twilight of pre-history. Even at the ripe age of 81, it is sad to lose one who brought so much fresh air and poetry into our literature. The kingdoms that he created will not pass away.[26]

CHAPTER TWO

Influences and Sources of the Ring Trilogy

*T**he Lord of the Rings*** is unarguably an imaginative feat of colossal proportions. But like other great literary works, it did not spring completely from its author's imagination. All writers are influenced by the world around them, their personal experiences, and the ideas they acquire from literature and other sources. And J.R.R. Tolkien was no exception. First, he lived through the turbulent first half of the twentieth century, during which the two most destructive wars in history occurred. He himself served in World War I and saw some of the slaughter firsthand. These events and experiences, along with others in his life, were bound to shape his worldview and, indirectly, color his writings.

In addition to these general influences, Tolkien drew several more specific ideas directly from existing literary sources. He was a learned scholar and linguist who read and absorbed hundreds of ancient and medieval European texts in their original, untranslated forms. These ranged from poems and fairy stories

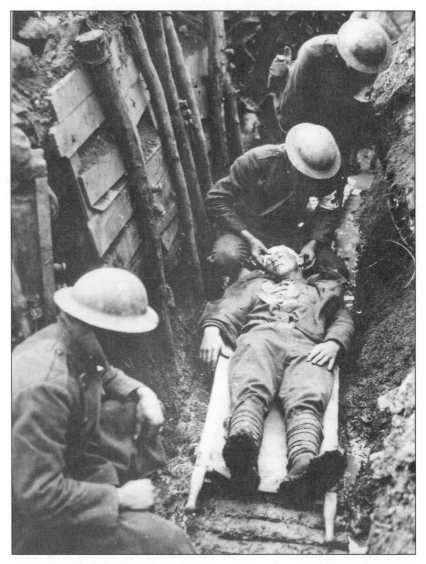

Tolkien knew first-hand about the horrors of trench warfare in World War I. His war experiences strongly influenced the descriptions of battles in his books.

to heroic myths and sagas in languages like Anglo-Saxon and Finnish. These sources fascinated him. And from many of them he borrowed the names of characters or places, as well as various events, situations, themes, and other ideas, for use in his monumental Ring trilogy. It is what Tolkien did with these many individual, mostly unconnected elements that continues to amaze and delight readers. He skillfully altered, interwove, and built on them, creating a rich new tapestry of mystery, heroism, danger, and adventure in a world strangely familiar yet never seen before.

General Influences

One way to be sure that a writer has been strongly influenced by a certain event or situation is if a work by that writer is allegorical. An allegory is a story that has a deeper meaning in addition to its surface meaning. Thus, any character, setting, event, or other element in an allegory may be a symbol that stands for and comments on something in the real world that exists outside the fictional world of the story.

In analyzing Tolkien's works, especially *The Lord of the Rings*, numerous modern literary critics have suggested that certain central characters, situations, and events in the writing are allegorical. For example, some have seen the evil conquests, killing, and devastation of the Dark Lord Sauron as symbolic of the conquests of the fascist dictators in World War II; in this scenario, the hobbits, Elves, men, and other races who oppose and eventually overcome Sauron's evil represent Britain, France, the United States, and other Allied forces. Other scholars have suggested that the events of *The Lord of the Rings* are an allegory of the triumph of "enlightened" Christianity over the "darker" forces of earlier pagan religions.

However, Tolkien himself insisted that such analyses of his great trilogy are mistaken. He strongly emphasized that he detested allegory, writing in 1964:

> I cordially dislike allegory in all its manifestations, and always have done so since I grew old and wary enough to detect its presence. I much prefer history, true or feigned [pretended], with its varied applicability to the thought and experience of readers. I think that many confuse

"applicability" with "allegory"; but the one resides in the freedom of the reader, and the other in the proposed domination of the author.[27]

By "applicability," Tolkien meant that both writers and readers could apply certain aspects of history to their understanding of a literary work. In other words, one could easily interpret a writing as being influenced by or a reaction to prior historical events, without its consciously symbolizing any specific event or events.

For example, for Tolkien, both World War I and World War II were frightening and traumatic events. And the horrors of war that he witnessed firsthand certainly influenced his written descriptions and imagery. An excellent example occurs in volume three, *The Return of the King,* when Sauron's evil followers lay siege to the city of Minas Tirith. Some of the devastation and suffering is reminiscent of the violence Tolkien had seen in the bloody trenches of World War I.

Some critics suggest that the reason for this is that Tolkien was at heart a traditionalist; he was, they say, an old-fashioned individual whose worldview was rooted in the late nineteenth century, a generally optimistic era that looked forward to the better world that industry and scientific progress promised to create in the next hundred years. But the twentieth century turned out to be the most violent and chaotic in history. And feeling let down, Tolkien reacted negatively to the onrush of a world that was too "modern" for his tastes and sensibilities. As literary scholar Chris Mooney puts it:

> *The Lord of the Rings* can be read as his response to modernity, to the world of catastrophic wars, terrible weapons, and industrialization that Tolkien felt was destroying his beloved rural, Edwardian England (represented in his books by the hobbits' peaceful, if parochial [provincial and narrow], homeland, "the Shire").[28]

One must be careful, however, not to read too much into Tolkien's general motives in writing the trilogy. This "negative response to modernity" model is valid only, Tolkien himself said, when it is applicable "to the thought and experience of the readers." In other words, many readers see the story as having relevance to the modern world because they personally relate to the book's characters and ideas. Tolkien himself insisted that he was simply trying to tell a good story that readers would enjoy. "The prime motive," he said,

> was the desire of a tale-teller to try his hand at a really long story that would hold the attention of readers, amuse them, delight them, and at times maybe excite them or deeply move them. . . . As for any inner meaning or "message," it has in the intention of the author none. It is neither allegorical nor topical.[29]

Fairy Stories and Myths

While the trilogy's general influences are open to interpretation and debate, Tolkien's more specific influences and sources are easier to trace. First, the story's setting—a fantasy world featuring strange races and creatures—is clearly based in large degree on the traditional genre of the fairy story. In its purist forms, it is a storytelling style rooted in the ancient and medieval folklore of northern Europe, having strong Celtic, Norse, Old English, and related elements. Its make-believe world is populated by witches, dragons, Dwarves, trolls, and other such beings, along with humans, all subject to the workings of magic and fate.

Tolkien, who was widely recognized as an expert on such lore, admitted that it is difficult to define the fairy story precisely. But in a now-famous 1938 lecture on the subject, he offered the following useful clues:

> Fairy stories are not in normal English usage stories *about* fairies or elves, but stories about . . . *Faërie*, the realm or state in which fairies have their being. *Faërie* contains many things besides elves, . . . dwarfs, witches,

trolls, giants, or dragons; it holds the seas, the sun, the moon, the sky; and the earth, and all things that are on it: tree and bird, water and stone, wine and bread, and ourselves, mortal men, when we are enchanted. . . . Most good "fairy stories" are about the *adventures* of

The genre of the fairy story heavily influenced Tolkien's writing. He pointed out that good fairy stories are about humans as well as supernatural folk.

men in the Perilous Realm [the dark and dangerous part of *Faërie*] or upon its shadowy marches. . . . [It is a place of magic], but it is magic of a peculiar mood and power, at the furthest pole from the vulgar devices of the laborious scientific magician. There is one proviso [required condition]. . . . The magic itself . . . [must] be taken seriously, neither laughed at or explained away.[30]

Tolkien was also aware that the fairy story is an offshoot or modified form of the myth, which is usually grander in scope and more serious in tone. Myths feature dragons, elves, and magic, too, but at their core resides the relationship between the gods and humans, especially heroes. Most often, the gods fight one another, or one or more human heroes manage to overcome tremendous obstacles, either aided or hindered by divine forces.

The Norse and German myths of Ragnarok, or "Twilight of the Gods," (in German called Götterdämmerung) constitute a classic example. In this classic tale, the good and evil members of an ancient superrace do mortal combat, destroying the earth's surface in the process; from the ashes, a new world is fated to rise. Echoes of this primeval battle can be detected in the mythology Tolkien created for Middle-earth. In the distant past, long before the days of Frodo and the other members of the Ring fellowship, a titanic conflict between the creators of the world toppled mountains and refigured continents; and from this catastrophe eventually emerged Middle-earth as it appears in the trilogy. Middle-earth itself is somewhat equivalent to Midgard, the realm of men in the old Norse legends.

Tolkien's approach, then, was to combine diverse elements of old northern European fairy stories and myths into a new, epic story with several fresh twists and emphases. "In *The Lord of the Rings*," remarks one of his biographers, Katharyn Crabbe,

we have a story that bridges the gap between fairy tale and myth. Though both elves and wizards and superhuman

An engraving depicts Ragnarok, the final battle of the gods in Norse legend. Tolkien drew on such myth in writing his tales of Middle-earth.

heroes are present, they are not quite central; instead, the story focuses on the fortunes of men and Hobbits. Yet the tone, [and] the importance of social issues . . . aspires toward the status of myth. This medial [middle-ground] position of the trilogy is reflected in Tolkien's treatment of his three great themes: the hero, the nature of good and evil, and the function of language.[31]

Tolkien's own statements supported such conclusions. He explained that he had, in fact, tried to integrate many different genres and influences. The goal in shaping the trilogy's story, he wrote, was

to make a body of more or less connected legend, ranging from the large and cosmogonic [having to do with the creation of the world] to the level of romantic fairy story, the larger founded on the lesser in contact with the Earth, the lesser drawing splendor from the vast backcloths which I could dedicate simply: To England; to my country. [The story] should possess the tone and quality that I desired, somewhat cool and clear, be redolent [suggestive] of our "air" (the climate and soil of the northwest, meaning Britain and the hither parts of Europe; not Italy or the Aegean, still less the East). And, while possessing (if I could achieve it) the fair elusive beauty that some call Celtic. . . . I would draw some of the great tales in fullness, and leave many only placed in the scheme, and sketched. The cycles [stories of individual races and characters] should be linked to a majestic whole.[32]

Of Dragons, Heroes, and Rings

To create this "majestic whole," Tolkien drew on many individual myths contained in old literary works. One of the more important of these was the Scandinavian *Elder Edda,* an anonymous compilation of myths dating from about A.D. 1300, which contains the legend of Ragnarok. A similar great battle, described in *The Silmarillion* and recalled in the Ring trilogy, is only one of dozens of elements Tolkien utilized in his writing. He also borrowed from the *Elder Edda* the names of many of the dwarves in the trilogy, as well as that of the great wizard, Gandalf.

One myth contained in the *Elder Edda*—one of the most famous in European lore—particularly inspired Tolkien. It is the story of a hero named Sigurth who slays a dragon, Fafnir, which guards a fabulous treasure belonging to an evil dwarf. Part of the treasure consists of some golden rings. The rings are cursed, and the dying Fafnir correctly predicts that they will eventually cause Sigurth's undoing.

Tolkien borrowed ideas not only from this version of the myth, but also from earlier and later versions. One of these is a more elaborate telling of the story that appears in the *Prose Edda* (or *Younger Edda*), by a thirteenth-century Icelandic chieftain, Snorri Sturluson. In this version, the hero, now called Sigurd, kills the dragon using a powerful sword. The weapon, which a god gave to Sigurd's father, had long been broken, but the young man had managed to piece it back together.

The original myth on which the dragon story in the two *Edda*s was based must have predated these works by many centuries. The proof is that still another version of the story appears in the Old English epic *Beowulf*, composed in about A.D. 700 by an unknown poet. One of its heroes is called Sigmund. *Beowulf* also contains references to several mythical races, among them

Beowulf prepares to slice off the monster Grendel's head in the famous Old English epic.

elves, giants, and orcs (monsters), all of which appear in *The Lord of the Rings*. Tolkien apparently derived several place names from *Beowulf* as well, including Mordor, his name for the evil land of the Dark Lord, Sauron. In *Beowulf*, the Anglo-Saxon word *morthor* is used to denote both murder and a place of torment and misery.

Perhaps the most famous version of the dragon-slayer myth, however, is a Teutonic epic, the *Nibelungenlied,* on which the nineteenth-century German composer Richard Wagner based his "Ring Cycle" of music dramas (operas). Sigurth/Sigurd/Sigmund has now become Siegfried. Like his counterparts in the other versions, he eventually dies, partly as a result of the curse carried by the rings he has stolen from the dwarf; also stolen from the dwarf, who was himself corrupted by the rings, is a cloak of invisibility. Eventually, Siegfried is avenged when his killers, too, are slain.

Anyone who has read Tolkien's Ring trilogy will be struck immediately by the number of ideas and characters it has in common with these earlier works. Reference is made in the trilogy to an earlier age when a dragon (Smaug) guarded a treasure. And of course, integral to the plot are the priceless rings, including the One Ring, which bears great powers, including that of making its owner invisible. But it also has the potential to corrupt and destroy. Like the dwarf in the myths, the creature Gollum has been completely corrupted by the Ring, which he calls "my precious." And after losing the object, he constantly tries to recover it. Another borrowed idea is the broken sword,

The hero Siegfried confronts death in the German version of the dragon-slayer myth.

which appears in the trilogy as an important royal symbol and heirloom guarded by Aragorn, the rightful king of Gondor.

Scouring the Old Sources

The elements considered so far are only a small portion of those Tolkien borrowed from old stories and myths. Another important medieval source he drew on was the *Gesta Danorum*, a history written in the twelfth century by a Dane named Saxo Grammaticus. One of the kings Saxo describes is a dragon killer, Frode, whose name is likely the source for Frodo, the chief hobbit hero of *The Lord of the Rings*. It should also be noted that in Saxo's account Frode is attended by Ygg, a mysterious prophet of undetermined age. Ygg strongly resembles the wizard

Gandalf, who befriends Frodo and accompanies him on the Ring quest. It is possible that Tolkien got Gandalf's name from the *Elder Edda* and his relationship with Frodo from Saxo's work.

Frodo and Gandalf are *major* characters in the trilogy. And Tolkien no doubt wanted to make sure that they resembled characters from old European legends; this imparted an air of authenticity and local color to the story. Yet he lavished no less care in scouring the old sources for names and images for *minor* characters and places. An excellent example is the legendary mariner Earendil. He was an ancient hero of the Elves whose story appears in a ballad recited by the hobbit Bilbo in *The Fellowship of the Ring*. Tolkien first ran across a form of the name Earendil—Earendel—in about 1913 in an old work he found while studying at Oxford. Titled *Crist of Cynewulf,* the work consisted of a group of old religious poems written in Anglo-Saxon. Two lines of the work read: "Hail Earendel, brightest of angels, above the middle-earth sent unto men." Long after reading these lines, Tolkien wrote, "I felt a curious thrill, as if something had stirred in me, half wakened from sleep. There was something very remote and strange and beautiful behind those words, if I could grasp it, far beyond ancient English."[33]

As it turned out, Earendel was a variant of Orwendel, an old German name for a bright star associated with a mythical hunter. Orwendel also appears in the *Prose Edda* and may be based on characters from ancient Greek and Hindu mythology.

About a year after he first encountered Earendel, Tolkien composed a poem based on him titled "The Voyage of Earendel the Evening Star." It began as follows:

Earendel sprang up from the Ocean's cup
   In the gloom of the mid-world's rim;
From the door of Night as a ray of light
   Leapt over the twilight brim,

And launching his bark like a silver spark

   From the golden-fading sand

Down the sunlit breath of Day's fiery death

   He sped from Westerland.[34]

This poem may well have marked the birth of the new mythology that Tolkien subsequently constructed as a background for his works about Middle-earth. In the trilogy, Earendil, like many other minor characters, adds detail, depth, and believability to the story. At one point, Bilbo sings of the long-dead mariner who built a boat with a timber hull and silver sails; this reminds the reader that the present inhabitants of Middle-earth have a rich past and folklore of their own. The trilogy's major characters therefore seem all the more complex and real. The passage also illustrates Tolkien's ability to translate effectively archaic verse into poetry that modern readers find elegant and plaintive.

What Makes the Work Great

The enormity of Tolkien's achievement becomes clear when one considers that Earendil and his voyage constitute just one of thousands of tiny pieces making up a vast mosaic. In a nutshell, that mosaic tells the story of an evil being named Sauron who attempts to enslave all the peoples of Middle-earth. To do so, he must possess and control the One Ring of Power. However, that object has fallen into the hands of Frodo the hobbit. Along with eight other heroes, who make up the Fellowship of the Ring, Frodo sets out on a quest to reach Sauron's kingdom of Mordor, where the hobbit intends to destroy the Ring by throwing it into the great volcano, Mount Doom. Sauron does everything he can to stop the ring bearers, who encounter many adventures and battles along the way. Finally, though, the Ring is destroyed in the fires of Mount Doom and Sauron's evil is eradicated.

This story has numerous subplots involving a multitude of imaginary races, characters, settings, and dangerous or charming events. *The Lord of the Rings* succeeds in part because many of these elements have a firm basis in the legends of the real world, especially those of the Norse, Germans, and other Europeans. And the skill with which the author bridges the gap between the real and the imaginary is what makes the work great.

CHAPTER THREE

The Major Characters and Races

The story of *The Lord of the Rings* deals primarily with the eternal struggle between good and evil. Accordingly, the main characters, along with the various races to which they belong, are generally divided into two groups—the good ones and the evil ones. Interestingly, though, most of the evil characters, including the most terrible of all—Sauron—started out good but were corrupted over time by one force or another. Tolkien realized that, even in the realm of fantasy, people and their personalities and motivations must not be portrayed simply as black and white, but in varying shades of gray. Thus, in the course of the story any good character is vulnerable to becoming a bad one at any given time, and sometimes evil characters betray other evil characters. These ominous possibilities should be kept in mind while examining the following list of the trilogy's principal characters. (For the sake of convenience, they are listed in alphabetical order, rather than by their importance.)

Aragorn, Boromir, and the Men

Aragorn and Boromir are both men hailing from the kingdom of Gondor. Men make up the youngest and most numerous of the major races of Middle-earth. In addition to Gondor, their kingdoms include Rohan and others, and their language, Mannish, is spoken by nearly all the races of Middle-earth. Of the many rings made by the evil Sauron, nine were given to men, who were corrupted by them and transformed into the ghastly Ringwraiths (or Nazgûl), his chief followers.

Of all the men in the story, Aragorn is the most important. Also called Strider, he first appears to Frodo and the hobbits in a tavern in the town of Bree. Frodo notices a strange man sitting at the table. As the hobbit approaches, the man throws back his hood, revealing a weather-beaten face highlighted by intelligent, piercing eyes.

As it turns out, Aragorn is the last chieftain of the Rangers of the North, descendants of the ancient inhabitants of the northern region of Gondor, who protect men, hobbits, and other peaceful races from the Dark Lord's armies. Aragorn was raised in secret by the Elven lord Elrond in Rivendell to keep him safe from Sauron. There, Aragorn learned his true identity—he was the rightful heir of Isildur, once king of Gondor (and he who took the Ring of Power from Sauron's hand). As he grew up, Aragorn learned much about ancient lore, herb craft, and healing. An expert swordsman, rider, huntsman, and tracker, he became the greatest traveler of his time and came to know all the lands and peoples of Middle-earth.

Having met Frodo and his companions in Bree, Aragorn becomes their guide and protector. When the group is attacked by the Ringwraiths and Frodo is badly wounded, it is Aragorn who drives the black riders away and keeps Frodo alive until the party reaches the Elven stronghold at Rivendell. At the Council of Elrond, Aragorn reveals that he is the rightful king of Gondor and swears to protect the ring bearer on the quest to destroy the Ring. Later, Aragorn collects an army and fights, along with men from Rohan, against Sauron's evil forces at Minas Tirith. When the men win their final victory over the minions of Mordor, Aragorn returns to his kingdom and claims the crown of his ancestors. Having fulfilled the promise of destroying the One Ring and ridding Middle-earth of Sauron, he marries and rules for many long years. When he finally dies, his followers lay him to rest in the Hall of Kings in Minas Tirith.

Boromir, the other man among the nine members of the Fellowship, is the son of Denethor, the last steward (acting king) of Gondor. Boromir's father had sent him to Rivendell to seek the meaning of a dream in which Boromir and his brother Faramir were advised to seek a broken sword. There, Boromir becomes a part of Elrond's council and volunteers to join the Fellowship.

Boromir is a born leader, powerful and skilled in combat after having fought in many wars against his country's enemies. He bears the family heirloom—the Great Horn, which if blown anywhere within the ancient boundaries of Gondor will summon help. While on the quest, the Ring's evil power begins to corrupt Boromir and he attempts to take the object from Frodo by force. Soon afterward, when the party is attacked by Orcs, Boromir, now free of the Ring's power, bravely fights to save Merry and Pippin. Finally pierced by many arrows, the man falls dead. In the eyes of his comrades, his demise atones for his terrible mistake of coveting the Ring, and they honor him by placing his body on a boat filled with the weapons of his many dead foes. The vessel passes through his homeland and is eventually swept out to sea.

Frodo and His Hobbit Friends

Frodo Baggins and his friends Sam, Merry, and Pippin make up the hobbit contingent of the Fellowship. The hobbits are one of the "civilized" races of Middle-earth. Their own history is a bit of a mystery even among themselves, and they long lived almost unnoticed by the other major peoples. Originally, the hobbits inhabited the land around the great river Anduin, between the Misty Mountains and Mirkwood Forest. But later they migrated westward and settled in the picturesque land that became known as the Shire.

The hobbits range from two to four feet in height. They are a peaceful, happy people who love good tilled earth, plain food, pipe-smoking, and drinking ale. They do not normally mingle with the other races and harbor a great distrust of anything or anyone new or different. Also, they love their home and disdain adventures of any sort. In addition, Tolkien writes, they wear brightly colored clothes but almost never wear shoes, mainly because they have big hairy feet with very tough soles. They are also graced with long nimble fingers that allow them to make many useful things. In some ways, Tolkien modeled the hobbits on himself, admitting in a 1958 letter:

> I am in fact a hobbit (in all but size). I like gardens, trees, and unmechanized farmlands; I smoke a pipe, and I like good plain food (unrefrigerated), but detest French cooking; I like, and even dare to wear in these dull days, ornamental waistcoats. I am fond of mushrooms (out of the field); have a very simple sense of humor (which even my appreciative critics find tiresome); I go to bed late and get up late (when possible). I do not travel much.[35]

Frodo is the chief hobbit in the Ring trilogy. His parents died when he was young and he was adopted by his cousin Bilbo Baggins, who found the One Ring after Gollum lost it. Frodo and Bilbo lived together in the village of Hobbiton until the time depicted in the opening of the trilogy. Bilbo has decided to leave the Shire and bequeaths Frodo his home and all his goods, including the Ring. Frodo subsequently becomes the ring bearer in the quest to destroy the object, and after the defeat of Sauron is allowed to accompany the Elves on their departure from Middle-earth for the mysterious land across the sea.

Frodo's faithful friend and servant, Sam (Samwise Gamgee), started out as a simple gardener who enjoyed spending his spare time sipping ale in local taverns. Sam joins the Fellowship and follows Frodo on the quest. During that journey, Sam demonstrates complete loyalty to his friend, saving him from injury or death on more than one occasion. After returning to the Shire at the conclusion of the great war, Sam works tirelessly to restore his homeland. He marries, fathers many children, and is eventually elected mayor of the Shire seven times. When, after many years, his beloved wife dies, he follows Frodo's path to the Grey Havens and journeys across the sea to join his friend.

The other two hobbits in the Fellowship, Pippin Took and Merry Brandybuck, are Frodo's and Sam's closest friends. In Rivendell, they insist on accompanying the others on the quest, and even though they are not warriors or Elf lords, the wizard Gandalf allows them to come along. One of Pippin's and Merry's most memorable experiences during the quest is their stay with Treebeard the Ent. After befriending the two diminutive characters, Treebeard gives them an Ent drink that makes them grow larger than any other hobbits.

When the two return to the Shire after the war, they lead their fellow hobbits to victory in the final battle against the forces of the former wizard Saruman. Later, both Pippin and Merry go on to have families of their own. And when both grow old, Aragorn, king of Gondor, asks them to return to his capital of Minas Tirith, where they eventually die and are laid to rest in great honor.

Gandalf the Grey

In appearance, Gandalf looks like an old man with white hair, a long white beard, a somewhat pointy nose, and piercing blue eyes. He wears a long cloak and a tall pointed hat with a wide brim. He is an Istari, or wizard, one of only five sent to Middle-earth long ago by the Valar (semidivine beings) to combat the Dark Lord. (Racially speaking, Gandalf is himself a Valar, but he takes the form of an old man while visiting Middle-earth.)

When Gandalf first arrived in Middle-earth, the Elven lord Círdan gave him Narya, one of the three Elven Rings of Power. Gandalf also served as a member of the White Council, a group of Elven lords and ladies headed by his superior wizard, Saruman.

Gandalf convinced the Dwarf lord, Thorin Oakenshield, to take Bilbo Baggins on the trip to the Lonely Mountain, an adventure told in *The Hobbit,* the prequel to the Ring trilogy. It was on this quest that Bilbo found the magical Ring Gollum had lost, an event that led directly to the situation described in the opening scenes of the trilogy.

Gandalf becomes the chief strategist and leader of the Fellowship of the Ring. During the quest, he fights a Balrog (ancient monster) on a stone bridge and falls along with the creature into the bowels of the earth when the bridge collapses. Gandalf is not lost, however. Later he reappears as Gandalf the White, ready to resume the quest to destroy the Ring. In fact, he proves instrumental in the victory over Saruman's army and casts Saruman out of the order of wizards. Gandalf also helps the armies of Gondor and Rohan achieve victory. And he rescues Frodo and Sam from death on the slopes of Mount Doom. With the defeat of Sauron, the great wizard's labors are finally finished. He joins Frodo and a group of Elves and departs Middle-earth at the Grey Havens, where his mission began more than two thousand years before.

Gimli the Dwarf

Gimli, an emissary to the Elves at Rivendell, joins the Fellowship as a representative of the Dwarves, a race nearly as ancient as the Elves. The Dwarves are sturdy, strong, and stout, standing about four to five feet high, and live an average of about 250 years. They are proud and quick to anger. They are also very industrious and hardworking; many among them show remarkable skill at working with metals and minerals. In fact, their extreme love of gold and jewels in the past often led to tragedies among them, and centuries ago they became mostly a wandering race whose numbers had been greatly reduced by war and a very low birthrate.

On the quest to destroy Sauron's One Ring, Gimli helps Gandalf lead the other members of the Fellowship through the Mines of Moria, the abandoned remnants of a once great Dwarf city. But it is in the land of Lorien that Gimli has his most memorable experience. There he meets the Elven queen Galadriel and becomes thoroughly enchanted by her beauty. Gimli also becomes fast friends with the Elf Legolas, never leaving his side during all the major battles of the War of the Ring.

After Sauron's defeat, Gimli leads a group of Dwarves to Minas Tirith to rebuild the gates. Then he settles in some caves in Rohan and eventually earns the title of Lord of the Glittering Caves. With the passing of Aragorn, Gimli rejoins his friend Legolas and the two sail over the sea, following in the footsteps of Frodo and Gandalf.

Gollum, a Lowly Creature

Gollum, or Sméagol as he was once known, was, like Frodo, once a ring bearer. It was Sméagol's cousin who found Sauron's evil Ring in the Great River long ago and was eventually murdered by Sméagol in his effort to obtain the object he thereafter called "my precious." In those days Sméagol was most likely a hobbit or perhaps a being very similar to one. But he slowly changed after fleeing with the Ring into the Misty Mountains. He burrowed deeper and deeper until he could go no farther into those dark depths, and his life became one of loneliness and shadow. For food, he killed fish in deep subterranean pools and ambushed small Orcs. Over time, his body and mind grew hideously twisted and he came to be called Gollum, after the guttural swallowing noises he now made.

After many years had passed, Gollum lost the Ring, which the hobbit Bilbo Baggins subsequently found. Unable to live without "my precious," the lowly creature left the mountains to find the one he was sure had stolen his Ring. Gollum was captured by the Elves but escaped and made his way into the land of Mordor. There he was again captured, this time by Sauron. Tortured mercilessly, Gollum finally told the Dark Lord about the Ring; its new owner, Bilbo Baggins; and the land of the Shire. Sauron then released Gollum, ordering him to find the Ring and return it to Mordor.

At the same time that the members of the Fellowship set out on the quest to destroy the Ring, Gollum becomes trapped in the Mines of Moria. But he soon sees this as a fortunate stroke of luck. The Fellowship passes through Moria and Gollum realizes that the Ring he covets is now in the possession of Frodo Baggins. The slithering creature carefully follows the ring bearer until the Fellowship breaks up. Then Frodo and Sam capture him and make him swear to serve the master of the Ring. Soon, however, the corrupt creature breaks his promise and arranges for Frodo and Sam to be ambushed by Shelob the spider.

Later, Gollum catches up with the two hobbits at the summit of Mount Doom. There, he bites off Frodo's finger to gain possession of the Ring. The creature cries out in triumph as he dances along the edge of the precipice. Seconds later, however, Gollum falls into the volcano's fiery crater, taking with him the object that had long obsessed him. Both he and the Ring are vaporized.

Legolas, Elrond, and the Elves

Legolas is an Elf of the Woodland Realm in Mirkwood, the largest forest in the western part of Middle-earth. Often called the "first born," the Elves were created by the Valar, the early semidivine race that shaped Middle-earth. The average Elf is about six feet tall, slender, graceful, and strong. Their senses of hearing and sight are far superior to those of men, and instead of sleeping, the Elves meditate on past ages and beautiful things.

Elves do not die naturally. Rather, they grow older slowly until they reach their desired age. However, they *can* be killed or, if they choose, can become mortal and die. Also, Elves do not as a rule seek any other races for friendship. However, long ago one group of Elves, the craftsmen of Eregion, were on extremely friendly terms with the Dwarves. Elves speak many languages, and over the course of many centuries they taught several other, younger races to speak and write. The greatest of the Elven languages, and the oldest tongue in all of Middle-earth, is called Quenya. (This was the first complete language invented by the young J.R.R. Tolkien.)

Legolas, who is proud of his Elven heritage, is sent to Rivendell as a messenger and there joins the Fellowship of the Ring. During the quest, he displays his amazing mastery of the bow, on several occasions shooting many arrows in rapid succession and with deadly accuracy. He also forms an unusually close and lasting friendship with Gimli the Dwarf. After the great War of the Ring, Legolas leads a group of Elves to Gondor to help restore the beauty of the realm. And following the death of Aragorn, Legolas and Gimli journey to the Grey Havens and embark on a one-way voyage across the great sea.

Another Elf who plays an important role in the story, Elrond, is a highly respected lord of great power and wisdom. He is a great healer and bears Vilya, the mightiest of the three Elven Rings of power. A principal foe of Sauron, Elrond labors tirelessly to rid the world not only of the Dark Lord, but of all evil. To that end, he convenes a great council in Rivendell, seeing to it that representatives of all the free peoples of Middle-earth attend. It is at this meeting that the decision is made to cast the One Ring into the fires of Mount Doom.

Elrond also decides that nine travelers will make up the Fellowship, choosing a member from each of the free races. During the War of the Ring, Elrond sends his Elves to fight against Sauron's evil hordes and also dispatches his own sons to help Aragorn. After the defeat of Sauron, Elrond departs from the Grey Havens for the mysterious land across the sea.

During their perilous journey toward Mordor, the companions of the Fellowship receive aid from another Elf—the Lady of the Woods, Galadriel. She is known for her beauty and wisdom. And like Elrond, she bears one of the three Elven Rings (this one known as Nenya). She also founded a secret Elven haven in the forest of Lorien and became its queen. When the companions of the Fellowship flee the Mines of Moria after their tragic encounter with the Balrog, they meet Galadriel and her Elves and she offers the travelers shelter and gifts. In turn, Frodo offers her the One Ring, but though tempted she refuses. Also like Elrond, at the end of the War of the Ring, Galadriel departs the Grey Havens and heads for the ancient Elven home across the sea.

Saruman, the Evil Wizard

Saruman the White was originally the leader of his order of wizards. Like Gandalf, he began as a foe of evil. But slowly, as Saruman's power and knowledge grew, so did his pride, and long ago he occupied the fortress of Isengard, with its ancient tower, Orthanc. It was there that he discovered many secrets that allowed his power to grow even more. Among these was a palantir, a magic crystal that established a link to the Dark Lord, Sauron, who thereby ensnared and converted Saruman to the cause of evil.

In the days of Frodo and the Fellowship of the Ring, Saruman makes war against his neighbors and destroys much of the surrounding countryside, including parts of the Fangorn Forest. This makes him the enemy of Treebeard the Ent. Subsequently, the evil wizard's army is defeated in the Battle of Hornburg and his fortress of Isengard is sacked by the Ents. Cast from the order of wizards by Gandalf, Saruman's only remaining powers are his cunning and wit, which he employs to persuade Treebeard to release him. Now free, he vents his fury on the hobbits, whom he blames for his defeat. Saruman oversees the devastation of large parts of the Shire until he is killed by his own servant, Grima Wormtongue. As Frodo and the other hobbits inspect the former wizard's body, they witness a strange mist rise up from it. Then a wind blows up from the west and disperses the mist until nothing is left. All that remains of Saruman is a layer of dried-out skin clinging to his skull.

Sauron, the Dark Lord

The Dark Lord Sauron was the ancient being who forged the great Ring of Power to rule all the other rings. This laid the groundwork for the war that finally ended with his defeat and the capture of the One Ring by Isildur of Gondor. Though Sauron's power had been diminished, he labored long in secret to seek revenge and find the Ring.

As the story of the trilogy begins, the Dark Lord has regained many of his lost powers and is beginning a new attempt to conquer Middle-earth. But he must have the One Ring to achieve ultimate power. Thanks to Gandalf, Frodo, and the other members of the Fellowship, Sauron is unable to regain possession of the fabulous object. When the Ring is finally destroyed in the fires of Mount Doom, so too is Sauron and all that was built or controlled by his evil powers. Sauron's chief servants are the nine Nazgûl (or Ringwraiths), whom he enslaved long ago. With his passing, they too are destroyed.

Treebeard and the Ents

A race of tree-herders, the Ents are perhaps nearly as ancient as the Elves who taught them to speak. The Ents age very slowly. And some, like Treebeard, were born not long after the creation of Middle-earth.

The physical presence of the Ents is arresting and fascinating, as revealed in the scene in which Merry and Pippin first encounter Treebeard, the leader of the Ents. They find themselves looking at an extremely unusual face belonging to what appears to be a combination of man, tree, and troll. The creature stands about fourteen feet high and has arms covered in a smooth brown skin. Finally, it has a beard with hairs that look like twigs at the roots and moss at the ends. Clearly then, one could walk by an Ent in the woods and not notice him.

Like other Ents, Treebeard is immensely strong. And he speaks Entish, a musical but slow and repetitive language that requires several days to conduct a single conversation. (No one other than an Ent has ever learned to speak it.) Treebeard learns from his new hobbit friends about the threat that the evil wizard Saruman poses. And the chief Ent rallies an Ent army that soon destroys the fortress of Isengard.

Treebeard and the Ents are unarguably among the most imaginative and entertaining characters in all of English literature. They, along with several other characters in *The Lord of the Rings,* testify to Tolkien's formidable creative powers.

CHAPTER FOUR

Major Themes Explored in the Trilogy

I n examining Tolkien's development of themes in the Ring trilogy, one is immediately struck by how much these themes resemble those of European mythology and medieval literary romances. This is not surprising. After all, Tolkien was at heart an old-fashioned medievalist whose main interests lay in the languages and literature of Europe's Middle Ages. The Norse, German, and Old English myths in which he immersed himself typically dealt with larger-than-life themes and characters: the ravages of war; the use and misuse of absolute power in the hands of gods, kings, and other supreme authorities; the hero's quest to overcome evil or oppression; and the positive qualities of loyalty, honor, and sacrifice. The narrative of *The Lord of the Rings* explores all of these themes, and others, often in graphic detail.

War Rooted in the Real World

Perhaps most graphic of all Tolkien's themes is his depiction of war. Consider an attack of Orcs and other dark forces against the battlements of men in *The Two Towers*. Rains of arrows glance off the stone walls, while the Orcs wave spears and swords. A battle trumpet sounds and the hideous creatures charge the walls and use a battering ram against the gate. This is not war as people know it today. There are no guns, or bombs, or tanks, or airplanes. Yet neither is it a made-up scene filled with fanciful and imaginary weapons and fighting. Rather, the rains of arrows, battle trumpet, and battering ram evoke a very real prior human age. "Here," noted scholar Norman F. Cantor writes, "is the medieval world at its most bellicose [warlike], destructive, and terrible moments: the Age of the Barbarian Invasions in the fifth and sixth centuries; the Hundred Years' War in the fourteenth and fifteenth centuries."[36]

Thus, Tolkien's depiction of castles, battlements, bows, catapults, sacked cities, and armed bands of soldiers threatening the tranquility of village societies is not fanciful. Even if the general setting—Middle-earth—and certain characters, such as Orcs and Elves, *are* imaginary, the general panorama of war he presents is a conventional and realistic reconstruction of medieval warfare. As a consequence, the reader finds him- or herself rooted in large degree in the real world. And that makes the experiences of the characters more identifiable and compelling.

Hero of the Common People

On the other hand, Tolkien's portrayal of the main hero of the War of the Ring—Frodo—is decidedly *un*conventional from a medieval standpoint. Most of the heroes in mythology are larger-than-life individuals who possess unusual physical and/or mental abilities, or have other traits that set their stature above that of the common people. It is not surprising, therefore, that they succeed in overcoming great odds, defeat powerful enemies, and reap rewards of happiness, glory, or eternal life.

By contrast, Frodo is anything but the image of the mythical hero. He is physically small and weak in comparison to men, Elves, and Orcs. He is also not unusually intelligent, of noble descent, or blessed with foresight or other special powers. For him, the quest of the Fellowship has less to do with overcoming the forces of evil and more with restoring peace and tranquility to the Shire and other lands threatened by violence and chaos. Frodo is not out to prove himself a great warrior or to achieve glory. All he really wants is to live quietly and modestly in his little corner of the world without fear or outside interference. In these respects, he is a common person championing a shared desire of all common people in history.

Another way that the development of the theme of heroism in Frodo's character is unconventional is how he is treated in the end. As Cantor points out, Frodo has saved the Shire, yet he does not achieve the notoriety and happiness normally expected of a hero. Instead, Tolkien writes in the final chapter of the trilogy that Frodo kept a low profile in the Shire and Sam was disturbed by how little attention people paid to the hero who had saved them and his adventures. According to Cantor:

> There are two ways to interpret this pessimistic conclusion to the long journey and great struggle. Tolkien is saying that in the modern world there are no rewards for heroes. They do not become kings; they become ailing veterans on abysmal pensions and fade away in loneliness and poverty. . . . Or Tolkien may be saying that this is the way it really was in the Middle Ages: not the Arthurian heroism of golden knights but the wearying, almost endless struggle of the little people against the reality of perpetual war and violent darkness to find a hiatus [break] of peace and security for their families and communities. *The Lord of the Rings* is thereby a medieval story, but a counter-romance, telling it "like it really was," not the way the court poets told it to flatter their lords.[37]

The Power of Friendship

Frodo's character is also a tool for exploring the themes of friendship and loyalty, which pervade the trilogy. Tolkien seems to tell his readers that in these qualities resides a power as great as or greater than that of wizards or magic rings. For the forces of love and loyalty provide hope in the face of despair, help bind the companions of the Fellowship in their common purpose, and ultimately prove more durable and potent than evil and betrayal.

From the very start, Tolkien establishes the feelings of love and friendship between the hobbit cousins, Bilbo and Frodo. This friendship between two very unlikely heroes (each of whom reluctantly embarks on epic adventures during his lifetime) endures to the end. After the Shire is restored to normalcy, they depart together from the Grey Havens on their final journey.

Friendship and loyalty are especially well developed in the steadfast and unerring devotion of Sam to Frodo. When Frodo tells Sam he is leaving the Shire on a dangerous mission and Sam insists on coming along, Frodo warns that neither of them is likely to make it back alive. But Sam insists that he will follow Frodo no matter where he goes, even to the moon. And if the Black Riders interfere, Sam will defend Frodo from them. Later, when Sam demands to go along on the Ring quest, Elrond the Elf recognizes his devotion to Frodo. Indeed, Sam remains at Frodo's side throughout most of the quest and risks all to rescue him from the Orcs. And it is with great sadness that Sam watches his friend sail away from the Grey Havens in the end.

Gimli the Dwarf and Legolas the Elf also become inseparable, remaining at each other's side during the quest. This is unusual because in the world Tolkien created most Elves do not care much for Dwarves. (The good relations between the Elves of Eregion and their Dwarf neighbors are an exception.) Moreover, Gimli and Legolas retain their close ties till the end of their lives. In the chronology of events Tolkien provides in volume three, he writes that in the year 1541 of the Fourth Age the two sailed together down a river to the sea and eventually the ship disappeared from sight, taking with it the last remains of the Fellowship of the Ring.

Loyalty is expressed in a different way in the sacrifice of Boromir (who dies fighting Orcs in an attempt to save Merry and Pippin), and in Aragorn's pledge to the dying Boromir. Here the loyalty is that of one man for another in a common cause—the salvation of their homeland and people.

Christian Themes

War and friendship lie more or less on the surface of the story and are therefore easily recognizable themes in the Ring trilogy. Less obvious are ideas derived from and reflecting the author's deeply held Christian beliefs. Tolkien himself insisted in a 1953 letter to a priest friend that the trilogy is "a fundamentally religious and Catholic work." However, he added this crucial qualification: "The religious element is absorbed into the story and the symbolism."[38]

Indeed, the religious ideas are "absorbed into the story" to such a degree that they are often difficult to find. As former Oxford University scholar T.A. Shippey points out, "There is almost no hint of any religious feeling at all in the characters or in their societies, not even where one would be most likely to expect it."[39] The hobbits get married, for instance, but no religious ceremonies are ever mentioned; nor are any churches described in the Shire. On the border of the human kingdom of Rohan looms a mountain called Halifirien, a term that probably comes from some Old English words meaning "Holy Mountain," yet the mountain has no marked religious significance in the story. Also, the men of Gondor revere the superhuman Valar, who helped create Middle-earth. However, as a race of powerful, semidivine beings, they are more akin to the pagan gods of the Greeks and Romans than to the single, all-powerful God of the Jews and Christians.

That Tolkien did not give the people and societies of Middle-earth outward and obvious Christian trappings is undoubtedly one of the strengths of the work. To have done so would have been to reproduce too overtly the society of medieval Europe; in that case, he may as well have made the story a historical romance set in seventh-century England or Germany. Instead, Tolkien chose to present what appears on the surface to be a faraway pagan society. Yet its peoples face some of the same moral dilemmas and choices that Christians have long wrestled with. And by describing these choices outside their familiar Christian setting, he shows that they are universal problems with which all thinking beings everywhere must contend.

Perhaps the most important of these is the moral dilemma of resisting temptation and the consequences of failing to do so. The fundamental exposition of this theme in the Judeo-Christian Bible is humanity's fall from grace in the Garden of Eden. God gives Adam and Eve free will. But they abuse it by giving in to temptation and disobeying God. The result is that their human descendants must constantly deal with the reality of evil, which they either give in to or resist. Similarly, in a past age Sauron was unable to resist the force of Morgoth's evil. Later, Gollum is unable to resist the temptation of possessing the powers of the One Ring, and as a result he becomes a corrupted, twisted creature. Both Sauron and Gollum suffer horrible deaths as punishment for their falls from grace. During the Ring quest, others are tempted by the Ring's powers, including Boromir and Frodo. Boromir pays for his transgression with his life, as he is pierced by Orc arrows; Frodo, on the other hand, ultimately suffers dejection, obscurity, and self-exile.

The Corruption of Power

The theme of temptation and the consequences of succumbing to it leads naturally to the most overriding and thoroughly explored theme of the entire trilogy: the corruption of power. Tolkien's central tenet, or guiding principle, is that unlimited power inevitably corrupts anyone who possesses it, even one who initially intends to use that power to good ends. Moreover,

"Tolkien does not simply tell us this once," scholars Agnes Perkins and Helen Hill write.

> A series of characters and incidents throughout the book explores the effects of power on characters strong and weak, good and evil, great and humble. He also shows us those to whom the possibility for power means nothing because they have removed themselves from the conflicts of the world. And finally, with the return of the true king, he shows us how power may come to one who has the inherited right but achieves it only after he has resisted the desire for unearned power. It is as though seeing the same gem from each of its many facets [angles], we perceive the same truth.[40]

First and foremost is the chief symbol of power and object of temptation and corruption—the One Ring. It can make its wearer invisible. It also keeps that person from aging. Furthermore, the One Ring has the ability to control the lesser rings, and through them the people who possess them. Finally, the desire to obtain and benefit from these powers is always too great for any being who bears the Ring; and ultimately, he or she will be tainted and corrupted by it.

The first mortal to be so corrupted was Isildur, the Gondorian king who in a past age cut the Ring from the hand of the defeated Sauron. Because the man refused to destroy the dangerous object, the ultimate victory of Elves and men over Sauron was thwarted. Later, Isildur's lust for power, as symbolized by his desire for the Ring, leads to his death. He is slain by Orcs and the Ring falls into the river Anduin, where another poor soul will find it and be destroyed in his turn.

Boromir's corruption by the Ring is not unlike Isildur's. Wishing to save his homeland by seeing the Ring destroyed, Boromir swears to serve and protect the ring bearer. But early on he feels the temptation to preserve and exploit the object; after all, if it is as powerful as people say, why not use it against Sauron?

Boromir urges Frodo to use the Ring as a weapon. However, Elrond the Elf admonishes Boromir, warning that the object's power is far too great for any person to handle without being corrupted by it. Boromir does not heed this warning. Instead, he attempts to force Frodo to give him the Ring.

The Perils of Self-Delusion

But before he can get his hands on the Ring and become further corrupted by it, Boromir dies in battle. In contrast, the character of Gollum shows the extent of the mental and physical effects of such corruption over a long period of time. Many years before, he murdered his cousin to get his hands on the Ring, and thereafter its evil powers further seduced and twisted him. In time, he became a slithering, slimy thing.

One might argue that Gollum started out as a person of average intelligence and perhaps less than average strength of will, so it is not all that surprising that he became corrupted by the Ring's power. In contrast, the case of the wizard Saruman the White presents an unexpected and much more contemptible example of absolute power corrupting absolutely. Saruman started out as an opponent of the Dark Lord but eventually allied himself with his enemy. The wizard's mistake was to think that he could avoid being corrupted if he used the powers he gained for his own "good" purposes, including betraying and defeating Sauron. Saruman even tries to seduce his fellow wizard Gandalf into this self-delusion.

But Gandalf is not deceived into thinking that the Ring can be used either safely or for good purposes. He knows that it can bring only corruption and evil, even to a being as lofty and enlightened as himself. In fact, early in the trilogy's first volume, when Frodo offered Gandalf the Ring, the wizard strongly expressed his own fear that it might seduce and corrupt him.

Saruman's corruption and ultimate destruction by absolute power and Gandalf's wise resistance to temptation concisely illustrate the theme of corruption that envelops and drives the story of *The Lord of the Rings.* Tolkien realized that the temptation to misuse great power has always been and remains a problem faced by kings, presidents, military generals, and other authority figures. And in the pages of his great and enduring epic, he provides both a warning of this danger and inspiring examples of how it can be avoided.

Notes

Introduction: The Author of the Century

1. Quoted in Alida Becker, ed., *A Tolkien Treasury*. Philadelphia: Courage, 2000, pp. 50–55.

2. Quoted in Chris Mooney, "Kicking the Hobbit," in Brandon Geist, ed., *The QPB Companion to* The Lord of the Rings. New York: Quality Paperback Book Club, 2001, p. 24.

3. Quoted in Katie de Koster, ed., *Readings on J.R.R. Tolkien*. San Diego: Greenhaven Press, 2000, p. 125.

4. Quoted in Michael Coren, *J.R.R. Tolkien, the Man Who Created* The Lord of the Rings. New York: Scholastic, 2001, p. 83.

5. Quoted in Geist, *QPB Companion*, pp. 17–18.

6. J.R.R. Tolkien, "Introduction," *The Fellowship of the Ring*. New York: Ballantine, 1965, p. xii.

7. Tolkien, "Introduction," *Fellowship of the Ring*, p. x.

8. Scott Rosenberg, "Introduction," in Geist, *QPB Companion*, p. 2.

Chapter 1: J.R.R. Tolkien's Life and Works

9. Quoted in Lin Carter, *Tolkien: A Look Behind* The Lord of the Rings. New York: Ballantine, 1969, p. 8.

10. Coren, *J.R.R. Tolkien*, p. 14.

11. Quoted in Humphrey Carpenter, *J.R.R. Tolkien: A Biography*. London: Allen and Unwin, 1977, pp. 22–23.

12. Quoted in Carpenter, *J.R.R. Tolkien*, pp. 36–37.

13. Quoted in Katharyn F. Crabbe, *J.R.R. Tolkien*. New York: Ungar, 1981, p. 7.

14. Quoted in Carpenter, *J.R.R. Tolkien*, p. 56.

15. Quoted in Carpenter, *J.R.R. Tolkien*, p. 56.

16. Quoted in Crabbe, *J.R.R. Tolkien*, p. 12.

17. Quoted in Carpenter, *J.R.R. Tolkien*, p. 59.

18. Quoted in Carpenter, *J.R.R. Tolkien*, p. 81.

19. Coren, *J.R.R. Tolkien*, p. 45.

20. Quoted in Carpenter, *J.R.R. Tolkien*, p. 172.

21. Quoted in Carpenter, *J.R.R. Tolkien,* pp. 180–81.

22. Quoted in Carpenter, *J.R.R. Tolkien,* p. 204.

23. Quoted in Carpenter, *J.R.R. Tolkien,* p. 204.

24. Quoted in Coren, *J.R.R. Tolkien,* p. 95.

25. Quoted in Coren, *J.R.R. Tolkien,* p. 95.

26. Quoted in Coren, *J.R.R. Tolkien,* pp. 124–25.

Chapter 2: Influences and Sources of the Ring Trilogy

27. Tolkien, "Introduction," *Fellowship of the Ring,* p. xi.

28. Mooney, "Kicking the Hobbit," p. 28.

29. Tolkien, "Introduction," *Fellowship of the Ring,* p. ix.

30. J.R.R. Tolkien, "On Fairy Stories," in *The Tolkien Reader.* New York: Ballantine, 1966, pp. 9–10.

31. Crabbe, *J.R.R. Tolkien,* p. 72.

32. Quoted in Carpenter, *J.R.R. Tolkien,* pp. 89–90.

33. Quoted in Carpenter, *J.R.R. Tolkien,* p. 64.

34. Quoted in Carpenter, *J.R.R. Tolkien,* p. 71.

Chapter 3: The Major Characters and Races

35. Quoted in Humphrey Carpenter, ed., *The Letters of J.R.R. Tolkien.* London: Allen and Unwin, 1981. Reprint, Boston: Houghton Mifflin, 2000, pp. 288–89.

Chapter 4: Major Themes Explored in the Trilogy

36. Norman F. Cantor, *Inventing the Middle Ages: The Lives, Works, and Ideas of Great Medievalists of the Twentieth Century.* New York: William Morrow, 1993, p. 228.

37. Cantor, *Inventing the Middle Ages,* pp. 228–29.

38. Quoted in Carpenter, *Letters of J.R.R. Tolkien,* p. 172.

39. T.A. Shippey, *J.R.R. Tolkien: The Author of the Century.* Boston: Houghton Mifflin, 2001, p. 175.

40. Agnes Perkins and Helen Hill, "The Corruption of Power," in Jared Lobdell, ed., *A Tolkien Compass.* La Salle, IL: Open Court, 1975, p. 58.

For Further Exploration

1. What was Tolkien's original reason for writing the Ring trilogy? When did he begin writing it? When was the work originally published?

2. Several of the major characters in Tolkien's Ring trilogy are hobbits. In some detail describe the hobbits as a race, including their physical appearance, likes and dislikes, and their homeland, the Shire.

3. In a letter cited in Chapter 3 of this volume, Tolkien explains how he modeled the hobbits partly on himself. In what ways are Tolkien and a typical hobbit alike?

4. Describe the wizard Gandalf. To what race does he belong and why did he come to Middle-earth? Describe his encounter with the Balrog in the Mines of Moria. What are Gandalf's major accomplishments in the story told in the trilogy? Where does he go after the conclusion of the War of the Ring?

5. What is the likely literary source from which Tolkien drew Frodo's name and Gandalf's image? From what source did he draw Gandalf's name?

6. What are some of the sources from which Tolkien borrowed the ideas of powerful, corrupting rings and a dragon guarding a treasure?

7. What is an allegory? Give an example of allegory that is often claimed by literary critics to exist in *The Lord of the Rings*. What strong evidence suggests that in fact this is not meant as allegory?

8. Among the most imaginative and colorful characters in *The Lord of the Rings* are the Ents. Provide a detailed physical description of an Ent. Why do the Ents decide to attack Isengard?

9. The most evil of all the characters in the trilogy is Sauron, the Dark Lord. How did he become evil? What is his chief goal? What object must he acquire to achieve that goal? How does that object stay out of his reach?

10. Besides Sauron, list and describe at least four other examples of characters from the trilogy who are partly or completely corrupted by various kinds of power. In each case explain how this happens.

11. Friendship and loyalty are major themes of the trilogy. List and describe at least three characters who strongly exhibit these qualities. List three characters who show an opposite trait—betrayal—and describe the circumstances in which these betrayals take place.

12. What is Aragorn's background and true identity? What is his ultimate goal? How does he achieve that goal? What happens to him at the end of his life?

13. Read Chapter 8, "The Scouring of the Shire," in the third book of the trilogy, *The Return of the King*. Then write an essay that explains in detail the devastation of the hobbit homeland that Frodo and his companions find when they return from their quest. How did this devastation come about? How do the hobbits counteract it?

14. Rent and watch the first of Peter Jackson's film adaptations of Tolkien's Ring trilogy—*The Fellowship of the Ring* (released in 2001). If you have read the original books, in general how true is the film to the first book? Cite some changes or deletions. Did any of these seriously detract from the story? Why or why not? How did the portrayals of the characters compare with the way you pictured them in your mind when reading the book? Were any characters less effective in the movie? Were any more effective? Why? If you had been the writer/director, would you have done anything different? If so, what and why?

Appendix of Criticism

Tolkien's Poverty of Invention?

This is an excerpt from American literary critic Edmund Wilson's 1956 review of Tolkien's trilogy, a negative critique that has since become famous for its lack of insight and foresight.

An overgrown fairy story, a philological curiosity—that is, then, what *The Lord of the Rings* really is. The pretentiousness is all on the part of Dr. Tolkien's infatuated admirers, and it is these pretensions that I would here assail. . . .

The Lord of the Rings . . . is indeed the tale of a Quest, but, to the reviewer, an extremely unrewarding one. The hero has no serious temptations; is lured by no insidious enchantments, perplexed by few problems. What we get is a simple confrontation—in more or less the traditional terms of British melodrama—of the Forces of Evil with the Forces of Good, the remote and alien villain with the plucky little home-grown hero. There are streaks of imagination: the ancient tree-spirits, the Ents, with their deep eyes, twiggy beards, rumbly voices; the Elves, whose nobility and beauty is elusive and not quite human. But even these are rather clumsily handled. There is never much development in the episodes; you simply go on getting more of the same thing. Dr. Tolkien has little skill at narrative and no instinct for literary form. The characters talk a story-book language that might have come out of [children's author] Howard Pyle, and as personalities they do not impose themselves. At the end of this long romance, I had still no conception of the wizard Gandalph, who is a cardinal [essential] figure, had never been able to visualize him at all. For the most part such characterizations as Dr. Tolkien is able to contrive are perfectly stereotyped: Frodo the good little Englishman, Samwise, his doglike servant, who talks lower-class and respectful, and never deserts his master. These characters who are no characters are involved in interminable adventures the poverty of invention displayed in which is, it seems to me, almost pathetic.

Edmund Wilson, "Oo, Those Awful Orcs,"
Nation, April 15, 1956, pp. 312–13.

Choosing the Books' Titles

These are excerpts from three letters Tolkien sent to his publisher, Rayner Unwin, in 1953. In these and other letters, Tolkien labored over choosing appropriate titles for the trilogy's three volumes.

March 24:
I have given some thought to the matter of sub-titles for the volumes, which you thought were desirable. But I do not find it easy, as the 'books', though they must be grouped in pairs, are not really paired; and the middle pair (III/IV) are not really related.

Would it not do if the 'book-titles' were used: e.g. *The Lord of the Rings:* Vol. I *The Ring Sets out* and *The Ring Goes South;* Vol. II *The Treason of Isengard,* and *The Ring goes East;* Vol. III *The War of the Ring,* and *The End of the Third Age?*

If not, I can at the moment think of nothing better than: I *The Shadow Grows* II *The Ring in the Shadow* III *The War of the Ring* or *The Return of the King.* JRRT. . . .

August 8:
I am . . . opposed to having separate titles for each of the volumes, and no over-all title. *The Lord of the Rings* is a good over-all title, I think, but it is not applicable specially to Volume I, indeed it is probably least suited to that volume. Except possibly in the matter of cost, I cannot see the objection to:

> *The Lord of the Rings.*   I The Return of the Shadow.
> "   "   "   "   " II The Shadow Lengthens.
> "   "   "   "   " III The Return of the King.

It is, surely, only by the use of a single over-all title that the confusion that you speak of can be certainly avoided.

I am not wedded to any of the suggested sub-titles; and wish they could be avoided. For it is really impossible to devise ones that correspond to the contents; since the division into two 'books' per volume is purely a matter of convenience with regard to length, and has no relation to the rhythm or ordering of the narrative. . . .

August 17:
I now suggest as titles of the *volumes,* under the over-all title *The Lord of the Rings:* Vol. I *The Fellowship of the Ring.* Vol. II *The Two Towers.* Vol. III *The War of the Ring* (or, if you still prefer that: *The Return of the King*).

The Fellowship of the Ring will do, I think; and fits well with the fact that the last chapter of the Volume is The Breaking of the Fellowship. *The Two Towers* gets as near as possible to finding a title to cover the widely divergent Books 3 and 4; and can be left ambiguous—it might refer to Isengard and Barad-dur, or to Minas Tirith and B; or Isengard and Cirith Ungol. On reflection I prefer for Vol. III *The War of the Ring,* since it gets in the Ring again; and also is more non-committal, and gives less hint about the turn of the story: the chapter titles have been chosen also to give away as little as possible in advance. But I am not set in my choice.

Humphrey Carpenter, ed., *The Letters of J.R.R. Tolkien.*
London: Allen and Unwin, 1981, pp. 167, 169–71.

The Origins of Hobbits?

Here, from his biography of Tolkien, scholar Daniel Grotta speculates on how the author of the Ring trilogy came up with the word hobbit.

Tolkien was never certain how he came to invent the word "hobbit." It was more spontaneous generation than calculation; certainly, not the combination of "rabbit" and (Thomas) "Hobbes," as the eminent American critic Edmund Wilson speculated. "I don't know where the word came from," admitted Tolkien. "You can't catch your mind out. It might have been associated with Sinclair Lewis' *Babbit.* Certainly not rabbit, as some people think. Babbit has the same bourgeois smugness that hobbits do. His world is the same limited place." Another theory on the origin of the word hobbit is advanced by Paul Kocher, author of *Master of Middle Earth.* According to Kocher, the Oxford English Dictionary defines the Middle English word "hob" (or "hobbe") as a rustic or a clown, a sort of Robin Goodfellow (the English equivalent of the "little people" of Celtic mythology). Since hobbits seem to display many of the characteristics of hobs—small size, simple nature, love of countryside,—then perhaps Tolkien unconsciously transformed a word with which he was undoubtedly familiar into a new creature. In any event, the word "hobbit" is uniquely Tolkien's invention, like "pandemonium" in Milton's *Paradise Lost* and "chortle" in Carroll's *Alice in Wonderland.*

> Daniel Grotta, *The Biography of J.R.R. Tolkien: Architect of Middle-Earth.* Philadelphia: Running Press, 1978.

Respect for the Natural World

Many scholars and critics have dissected Tolkien's Ring trilogy, looking for themes, symbols, and social or political commentary. Some of these explorations are more credible and insightful than others. Among the more thoughtful examples of early Tolkien criticism is this 1972 tract examining the work from an environmentalist's point of view.

In Tolkien's world, respect is paid not only to other "races" but to living things generally. Perhaps the most important problem in the latter half of the twentieth century is presented by the natural environment, ravaged by possessive men in search of wealth and power. In the Trilogy, the evil beings are connected with such desecration; Saruman and Sauron both attack the natural organic world, leveling forests, covering vegetation with ash-piles, factories and their waste, the "produce" of slave-worked mines. But those who fight against evil respect the natural world, as guardians of all created beings. The ents care for their trees, the dwarves for their gleaming minerals. Aragorn finds help for wounds in the *athelas,* a wild herb. Sam grows an elven tree, the *Mallorn,* far from its home in Lorien.

The imagination requires that even plants be permitted their own natures, and shown care rather than possessiveness. This general respect for all created life in *The Lord of the Rings* speaks to those among us who fear the disappearance of redwoods and whales, mountain wilderness and hidden seashores to serve society's destructive needs. If we try to turn every mountain valley into a national park with camping areas, general stores and play grounds, we have remade it in our image, and so extended a step further "the drab blur of triteness or familiarity" which must ultimately threaten our own necessary sense of wonder at other forms of life. And under our heavy hand, such unique life can be extinguished. *Care for the world* might be the theme of Tolkien's Trilogy.

Nor does the Imagination deny the existence of evil. Our society can be accused of hiding reality under its images: the glossy prints of the large-circulation magazines or the smiling caricatures of housewives discovering a new soap in television commercials. Distress is smoothed away, and suffering denied not only existence but value. People hurt, however; they suffer from poverty, hunger, loneliness, fear and a long list of human symptoms which no soap product or movie star can cure. They also suffer from the absence of great causes for which to suffer, paradoxical as that may seem. In Tolkien's fantasy, we do not escape from evil: there is no running away from the Shadow of Sauron. The ways in which created beings respond to the challenge such power presents distinguish them; make them more complex in nature than we think at first; make them moral. For a reader tired of seeing human beings as only partial figures caught in the conventions of social life and prescribed rituals, the revelation of hidden natures available for good or evil is valuable.

Robley Evans, *J.R.R. Tolkien*. New York: Crowell, 1972.

Realities That Determine the Story

In this excerpt from his recent study of Tolkien's writings, literary scholar T.A. Shippey summarizes the three central facts concerning the One Ring, as told to Frodo by Gandalf. These are the realities that determine the story, Shippey says, without which it would not be believable.

At the heart of *The Lord of the Rings* are the assertions which Gandalf makes in Book I/2, his long conversation with Frodo. If they are not accepted, then the whole point of the story collapses. And these assertions are in essence three. First, Gandalf says that the Ring is immensely powerful, in the right or the wrong hands. If Sauron regains it, then he will be invincible at least for the foreseeable future: 'If he recovers it, then he will command [all the other Rings of Power] again, even the Three [held by the elves], and all that has been wrought with them will be laid bare, and he will be stronger than ever.' Second, though, Gandalf insists that the Ring is deadly dangerous to all its possessors: it will take them over, 'devour' them, 'possess' them. The process may be long or short, depending on how 'strong or well-meaning' the possessor may be, but 'neither strength nor good purpose will last—sooner or later the dark power will devour him'. Furthermore this will not be just a physical take-over. The Ring turns everything to evil, including its wearers. There is no one who can be trusted to use it, even in the right hands, for good purposes: there are no right hands, and all good purposes will turn bad if reached through the Ring. Elrond repeats this assertion later on, 'I will not take the Ring', as does Galadriel, 'I will diminish, and go into the West, and remain Galadriel'. But finally, and this third point is one which Gandalf has to re-emphasize strongly and against opposition in 'The Council of Elrond', the Ring cannot simply be left unused, put aside, thrown away: it has to be destroyed, and the only place where it can be destroyed is the place of its fabrication, Orodruin, the Cracks of Doom.

These assertions determine the story. It becomes, as has often been noted, not a quest but an anti-quest, whose goal is not to find or regain something but to reject and destroy something. Nor can there be any half-measures, attractive as these may seem. Gandalf will not take it, Galadriel will not take it, it would be disastrous to take it to Gondor, as Boromir and Denethor would prefer. One might point out that while all this is perfectly logical, granted the initial assumptions, Gandalf's basic postulates might take a bit of swallowing. Why should we believe them? However, while critics have found fault with almost everything about *The Lord of the Rings*, on one pretext or another, no one to my knowledge has ever quibbled with what Gandalf says about the Ring. It is far too plausible, and too recognizable. It would not have been so before the many bitter experiences of the twentieth century.

> T.A. Shippey, *J.R.R. Tolkien: The Author of the Century.*
> Boston: Houghton Mifflin, 2001, pp. 113–15.

Tolkien the Medievalist

In the following excerpt, medieval European scholar Norman F. Cantor explains that he greatly admires Tolkien for bringing some of the realities of medieval society to life in The Lord of the Rings.

The Lord of the Rings does in indelible fashion capture three salient [important] aspects of medieval civilization. First, it communicates the experience of endemic war and the fear of armed bands that was a frequent condition of the period from 400 to the middle of the eleventh century and again from about 1290 to the late fifteenth century. The dark force of incipient terrorism [the first acts of terrorism] in the form of armed invasion was a constant threat and fell particulary on village society, the common people. This is communicated in *Rings* in a dramatic fashion that no conventional historical exposition can come close to matching.

Secondly, *Rings* makes us feel the circumstances and conditions of a long journey undertaken not by a great nobleman with a powerful retinue [group of military followers] by an ordinary soldier with two or three companions. This kind of distant journeying by obscure people over long distances, for one reason or another, we know from stray references, was a much more common occurrence at all times in the Middle Ages, but especially after 1100, than we might a priori predict from the kind of primitive transportation system the medievals had access to. People of modest social status in surprising numbers traveled long distances, mostly on foot. This is a strange fact of medieval life, and *Rings* is centered on this event. Tolkien convinces us that the way this happened was that some local village leader got it into his head that he had to do something to help or save his people, something had to be carried a very long distance, some contact vaguely imagined had to be made, and off the person and two or three companions went on their incredibly long, footsore journey. These journeys were rarely documented for us in the Middle Ages and almost never in detail. Tolkien, by imagining such a journey, has graphically re-created an important but poorly understood facet [aspect] of medieval social life.

Thirdly, Tolkien stresses for us what [author] C.S. Lewis also believed: that medieval heroism was not a special manifestation of aristocratic culture but something that existed among people of relatively humble social status. There is something very English about this conviction that the little people of the medieval world were heroic, too. However, not only is it a product of the Edwardian sentimental retromedieval imagination, but it has some documentation in the known realities of medieval English history. From 1194 onward . . . there is available to us an increasingly detailed record of litigation [lawsuits] in the county courts, and most of the "pleaders," as they were called, were strictly local people, small landowners, not the magnates, not the grand nobility. By the fourteenth century these records of litigation in the county courts allow us to look into the lives and feelings of the little people of the countryside—the lesser gentry and the yeoman [a person who owns and cultivates a small farm] class. They turn out to be highly articulate, self-conscious, ambitious, intelligent, the instigators of capitalist rationality. No other series of records from medieval Europe, before Florence of the fifteenth century, gives us such detailed insight into the minds of ordinary country or urban society. There are the Frodo types, socially. Thus Tolkien's reconstruction of the mentality of these kinds of people coincides with the evidence from the records of the common law. In this regard Tolkien is . . . an archaeologist of medieval society.

> Norman F. Cantor, *Inventing the Middle Ages:*
> *The Lives, Works, and Ideas of Great Medievalists*
> *of the Twentieth Century.* New York: William
> Morrow, 1993, pp. 231–32.

Tolkien Reacts to the Twentieth Century

As award-winning science-fiction writer Michael Swanwick asserts here, much of the content of Tolkien's Ring trilogy can be seen as a negative reaction to the many violent and chaotic events of the first half of the twentieth century.

When I reread the Ring trilogy after many years, I dicovered that the single best adventure story ever written . . . had transformed itself into something else entirely. It was now the saddest book in the world. This is a tale in which everyone is in the process of losing everything they hold most dear. The elves, emblematic of magic, are passing away from Middle-earth. Galadriel laments the dwindling of Lothlorien. Treebeard reveals that ents are surrendering their awareness and growing increasingly tree-ish. The old ways—all of them—are disappearing. Trees are being cut down, and streams defiled. Blasting powder has been invented. Industrialization is on its way. Defeating the Dark Lord and slaughtering his armies will not change any of this.

Tolkien was quite rightly scornful of those who tried to read allegorical intent in his work. But absence of allegory does not equal lack of relevance. . . . To read Sauron as [Nazi dictator Adolf] Hitler and the Ring as the atom bomb is to reduce a significant work to triviality. Yet Tolkien fought in World War I and he wrote much of his masterpiece during the darkest reaches of the second [World War II]. The England of his youth was thoroughly gone by then. Like most of his generation, he mourned its passing. His portrayal of evil events was informed by things he knew only too well: Hitler, [Italian dictator Benito] Mussolini, [Soviet dictator Joseph] Stalin, the bomb, genocide, gas warfare, cultural homogenization, the Corporate State, depersonalization, pollution, mind control, the Big Lie . . . all the ills of his times are implicit in his work.

From experience, Tolkien knew that there are only two possible responses to the ending of an age. You can try to hold on, or you can let go. Those who try to seize the power to ward off change are corrupted by despair (Saruman, Theoden, and Denethor most notably, but there are others). Those who are willing to pay for all they have, to suffer and make sacrifices, to toil selflessly and honorably, and then to surrender their authority over what remains, ultimately gain the satisfaction of knowing that the world has a future worth passing on to their children. But it has no place for them anymore. Nevertheless—and this is what moved me most—Tolkien's vision of the combined horrors of the twentieth century ended with hope and forgiveness.

This is a book sad with wisdom.

Michael Swanwick, "A Changeling Returns,"
in Karen Haber, ed., *Meditations on Middle-Earth*.
New York: St. Martin's Press, 2001, pp. 35–37.

Many Imitators, but No Equals

Like many modern writers, award-winning novelist Lisa Goldstein admits to feeling Tolkien's influence. Here she comments on how Tolkien's Ring trilogy not only inspired writers like herself, but also spawned numerous imitators, none of whom could surpass the original.

After I read *The Lord of the Rings,* I looked around for more of the same. At the time there seemed to be very little that provided the same thrill: some children's books, the Earthsea series, Lin Carter's amazing Ballantine Adult Fantasy series. Finally, at the end of the seventies, a number of books came out that were strongly influenced by *The Lord of the Rings.*

"Strongly influenced" may be understatement; there are scenes in at least one of these that seem to have been lifted in whole from Tolkien. I was working in a bookstore when this book came out, and I was very excited at the advanced publicity. As I said, I was starved for fantasy, and there are only so many times you can reread Tolkien. We ordered a display, what publishers call a "dump" (which gives you some idea of how publishers feel toward their books), containing, I think, eighteen copies. I got an advanced reading copy, settled down to be enchanted, and found myself reading a pale imitation of *The Lord of the Rings.*

I once felt very bitter toward this book; I thought (and still think, somewhat), that it is at least partly to blame for all the cheap tripe that came later. Now, though, I have a different view, a view I incline to in my less cynical moments. A myth is a story of a hero's journey into darkness, and his or her return. All myths are the same in this way; it is only the trappings that are different. Perhaps the author of this book, like all of us, was moved by this story, and moved to retell it; perhaps in retelling it he was more like a bard [storyteller or poet] of old, singing a story he had heard to a transfixed audience around a fire. Myths were once told and retold, changed and rechanged; intellectual property is a fairly recent concept. That he proved to be such a poor bard compared to the master does not change the nature of the tale.

But when I read my advanced copy I despaired, and not just because I thought the book was derivative and the language clunky. I feared that no one would buy this thing, that we had ordered far too many copies and that they would all have to be returned, with us paying the postage on what was, after all, a fairly hefty tome (though nothing like the toe-crushers that followed). The bookstore had just opened, and a little thing like postage was a huge expense in those days.

To my absolute surprise, the book began to sell, and sold without ceasing. We got rid of the entire dump and had to pick up more copies at our local book distributor. I was in a bit of a quandary [dilemma], though, when our customers asked me if it was any good, and ended up saying something like, "If one of the things you enjoyed about Tolkien was his language, you won't like this. But if you read Tolkien only for the story, you will find this very much like that, maybe too much so." To a man and a woman, they bought the book.

Then the floodgates opened. Hundreds of epic fantasies, maybe even thousands, have been published since then. People realized that they could write them without paying attention to style, that they didn't have to spend decades building a world, but could make one out of cheap cardboard, or, even simpler, could borrow it from a better writer. Some of these books were so bad they wouldn't even make decent landfill. And these, too, were bought and eagerly devoured.

It's the story: the story is the important thing. People are so hungry for these tales that they will read them and make them best-sellers no matter how badly written they are. Some of them are poor retellings, but such is the power of the hero's journey that people will read them anyway.

Lisa Goldstein, "The Myth-Maker," in Karen Haber, ed., *Meditations on Middle-Earth.* New York: St. Martin's Press, 2001, pp. 194–96.

Age of the Geeks?

In this entertaining tract, Julian Dibbell makes the point that so-called geeks have contributed significantly to the phenomenal popularity of Tolkien's Ring trilogy and that in recent years, members of this highly educated, technologically proficient, and decidedly "Tolkienesque" subculture have increasingly come to shape the norms of the computer age.

In 1961, five years after publication of the final volume in John Ronald Reuel Tolkien's three-part fantasy epic, *The Lord of the Rings,* the formidable English literary critic Philip Toynbee announced with great relief that popular enthusiasm for Tolkien was now thoroughly tapped out and his works were finally on their way to "merciful oblivion." Nice call, Phil: Four years later, the first American paperback edition of *The Lord of the Rings* appeared, and the modestly best-selling book—the tale of brave little hobbit Frodo Baggins's quest to destroy the Ring of Power and save Middle Earth from the Dark Lord Sauron—blew up to a youth-cultural legend. Three million copies were sold between 1965 and 1968. . . . [Moreover] the year 2001 finds Tolkien's following bigger and busier than any other period in the four decades since Philip Toynbee wrote its obituary.

What that amounts to in the greater pop cultural scheme of things, of course, is harder to say than it used to be. Back in the days when Tolkien was still alive and in the habit of referring to his shaggy, puff-sleeved fans as "my deplorable cultus" (he was a straitlaced, archconservative Catholic himself), they were easily mistaken for flower children, or at least fellow travelers on the road to a global transformation of consciousness through drugs, electrified music, and other forms of postindustrial enchantment. But now that the world-historical context has simmered down and a somewhat tamer generation has filled out the hobbit-loving ranks, everyone can see they're just geeks.

Or something even geekier, arguably: ur-geeks. Keepers of the geek flame. For if *The Lord of the Rings* is not the sine qua non [essential artifact] of geek culture, it's hard to think what is. After all, the the vast genre of fantasy fiction is, along with sci-fi, one of the two great narrative flows feeding the Nerd Nation's imaginative life, and nobody doubts that Tolkien single-handedly invented it. And that's not even counting the immense subcultural continent that is Dungeons & Dragons and every role-playing game descended from it—from the complex, online timesuck EverQuest to the Japanimated children's saga DragonBallZ—all of which testify to the formative influence of the Tolkien mythos. Throw in *Star Wars* (as Tolkienesque a space opera as ever there was) and the argument is pretty much a lock: Without the lucidly imagined geography of Middle Earth and the archetypal characters Tolkien stocked it with—the grave wizards, stout dwarves, evil orcs, and above all, plucky, permanently adolescent hobbits—geekdom as we know it would simply not exist.

If you feel that's no particularly meaningful achievement, I understand. But maybe you could indulge me and imagine, just for a moment, that the fact that we live in a world increasingly made by geeks actually makes their collective imagination worth understanding. Think about computers, their evolution shaped by a hacker culture that insisted some of the earliest dot-matrix printers be programmed to produce the elvish Fëanorian script. Think about the Internet, whose founding architects included the D&D fanatic who created the Adventure, the very first, very Tolkienized online role-playing game. Think, for a moment, about these profoundly transformative technologies. And then consider the possibility that the structures of feeling we inherit from them might just have some intimate connection to the dream life of the people who designed them. Consider, in other words, the possibility that *The Lord of the Rings*, geek culture's defining literary creation, might just be one of the defining literary creations of our age.

Julian Dibbell, "Lord of the Geeks," in Brandon Geist,
ed., *The QPB Companion to* The Lord of the Rings.
New York: Quality Paperback Book Club, 2001, pp. 69–71.

Chronology

1892
On January 3, John Ronald Reuel Tolkien is born in Bloemfontein, South Africa.

1895
Tolkien travels to England with his mother, Mabel, and brother, Hilary. The following year, Tolkien's father dies in South Africa.

1900
Tolkien begins attending King Edward's School in Birmingham, England.

1904
Mabel Tolkien dies.

1910
Tolkien is accepted to the prestigious Oxford University.

1916
Tolkien marries his longtime sweetheart, Edith Bratt. He serves in France during the height of World War I; in November, he is sent home to England to recover from "trench fever."

1917
Tolkien's eldest son, John, is born.

1920
Tolkien is appointed reader in English at the University of Leeds. His second son, Michael, is born.

1922
Tolkien publishes his first major literary work, *A Middle English Vocabulary*.

1924
Tolkien's youngest son, Christopher, is born. Tolkien works on his own edition of the medieval romance *Sir Gawain and the Green Knight*, which he publishes the following year.

1926
Tolkien meets and becomes friends with noted English professor and writer C.S. Lewis.

1929
Edith gives birth to the Tolkiens' only daughter, Priscilla.

1936
Tolkien finishes the manuscript of *The Hobbit* and it is accepted by London publisher Allen and Unwin.

1937

The Hobbit is published and publisher Stanley Unwin suggests that Tolkien write a sequel. Soon, Tolkien begins work on the story that will eventually become the great trilogy *The Lord of the Rings*.

1945

Tolkien becomes Merton Professor of English Language and Literature at Oxford University.

1949–1950

Tolkien finishes *The Lord of the Rings*.

1954–1955

Allen and Unwin publishes the trilogy.

1959

Tolkien retires from his professorship.

1965

Ballantine Books releases a revised edition of the trilogy, which quickly becomes a cult classic, especially in the United States.

1971

Edith Tolkien dies at age eighty-two.

1973

On September 2, J.R.R. Tolkien dies at age eighty-one.

1977

Another Oxford University alumnus, scholar Humphrey Carpenter, publishes the definitive biography of Tolkien; Christopher Tolkien publishes *The Silmarillion*, which he has completed and edited for his father.

1996

An English poll of twenty-six thousand readers names *The Lord of the Rings* the greatest literary work of the twentieth century.

2001

The Fellowship of the Ring, the first of director Peter Jackson's big-budget films of Tolkien's Ring trilogy, is released to wide acclaim; the second and third films are released in 2002 and 2003.

Works Consulted

Major Works by J.R.R. Tolkien

The Hobbit. New York: Ballantine, 1966. Tolkien's first published work about the races and characters of Middle-earth and the prequel to the Ring trilogy, *The Hobbit* focuses on the adventures of Bilbo Baggins and how he acquired the One Ring of Power. It can be summed up in one word: delightful. It is advisable to read this book before tackling the larger trilogy.

The Letters of J.R.R. Tolkien. Ed. Humphrey Carpenter. London: Allen and Unwin, 1981. Reprint, Boston: Houghton Mifflin, 2000. Serious Tolkien fans and buffs will be fascinated by part or all of this large collection of letters written by Tolkien over the course of his adult life.

The Lord of the Rings:
Vol. 1: *The Fellowship of the Ring.* New York: Ballantine, 1965.
Vol. 2: *The Two Towers.* New York: Ballantine, 1965.
Vol. 3: *The Return of the King.* New York: Ballantine, 1965.

Note: The 1965 Ballantine edition of the trilogy was the first revised version of the original edition, published by Allen and Unwin (London) in 1954–1955. Allen and Unwin published its own revised edition in 1966; later came a 1987 edition by Houghton Mifflin (Boston) and one by HarperCollins (London) in 1994. Each of these editions went through many printings. In 2001 and 2002, Houghton Mifflin and other publishers released new editions to coincide with the release of director Peter Jackson's first two feature films of the trilogy.

Poems from the Hobbit. Boston: Houghton Mifflin, 1999. An entertaining compilation of poetry and riddles from Tolkien's Middle-earth mythos.

The Silmarillion. Ed. Christopher Tolkien. London: Allen and Unwin, 1977. Tolkien's grand vision of the long history and mythology of Middle-earth, finished by his son Christopher, is not for the casual fan of the latest Tolkien calendar or movie. This is a serious, challenging, epic work of mythology that is, in style, intent, and comprehensiveness, comparable to the Bible and Homer's *Iliad* (though not as important as these works from a literary/historical standpoint). A must for true Tolkien fans.

The Tolkien Reader. New York: Ballantine, 1966. Contains Tolkien's "Leaf of Niggle," *Farmer Giles of Ham, The Adventures of Tom Bombadil,* and his noted 1938 essay on the form and values of fairy stories.

Analysis and Criticism of *The Lord of the Rings*

Jane Chance, *The Lord of the Rings: The Mythology of Power.* Lexington: University Press of Kentucky, 2001. Discusses Tolkien's use of politics and language as they relate to the acquisition of great power. Somewhat esoteric and not completely fresh as Tolkien criticism goes, but still thoughtful and worthwhile, especially for those who are first getting to know Tolkien's works.

Karen Haber, ed., *Meditations on Middle-Earth.* New York: St. Martin's Press, 2001. A collection of recent critical commentary by writers ranging from Raymond Feist and Poul Anderson to Ursula K. Le Guin and Orson Scott Card.

David Harvey, *The Song of Middle-Earth: J.R.R. Tolkien's Themes, Symbols, and Myths.* London: Allen and Unwin, 1985. An excellent discussion of how Tolkien developed the major themes of his works.

Neil D. Isaacs and Rose A. Zimbardo, eds., *Tolkien: New Critical Perspectives.* Lexington: University Press of Kentucky, 1981. Now dated, these essays about Tolkien's works are still valuable for students and others approaching Tolkien for the first time.

Jared Lobdell, *England and Always: Tolkien's World of the Rings.* Grand Rapids, MI: Eerdman's, 1982. One of the very best collections of Tolkien commentary. Highly recommended.

Brian Rosebury, *Tolkien: A Critical Assessment.* New York: St. Martin's Press, 1992. One of the best available volumes of analysis of Tolkien's works. Highly recommended.

T.A. Shippey, *J.R.R. Tolkien: The Author of the Century.* Boston: Houghton Mifflin, 2001. Largely rehashes much earlier Tolkien criticism, especially from Shippey's own insightful 1983 book, *The Road to Middle-Earth* (Boston: Houghton Mifflin). However, for those who have not read the earlier work, this is a solid introduction to analysis of Tolkien, including Shippey's emphasis (disputed by some) that most of Tolkien's sources were Anglo-Saxon.

About J.R.R. Tolkien

Humphrey Carpenter, *J.R.R. Tolkien: A Biography.* London: Allen and Unwin, 1977. Widely acknowledged as the most complete and reliable biography of Tolkien. Includes numerous quotes by and about Tolkien from letters, diaries, newspapers, and other sources. Highly recommended for serious students of Tolkien.

Michael Coren, *J.R.R. Tolkien: The Man Who Created* The Lord of the Rings. New York: Scholastic, 2001. Though brief and written for high school students, this is a useful overview of Tolkien's main experiences and achievements.

Katharyn F. Crabbe, *J.R.R. Tolkien*. New York: Ungar, 1981. A commendable short biography of Tolkien. Contains some interesting brief commentary of his main works.

Charles W.R.D. Moseley, *J.R.R. Tolkien*. Plymouth, UK: Northcote House, 1997. A very well-researched and well-written introduction to Tolkien's life and works, with a considerable amount of worthwhile commentary about his "sub-creation" of highly detailed races and kingdoms.

Guides to Tolkien's Works

Robert Foster, *The Complete Guide to Middle-Earth: From* The Hobbit *to* The Silmarillion. New York: Ballantine, 1978. Recognized by many Tolkien fans as the best general guide to his works, this is very comprehensive and detailed. Highly recommended.

James H. Gillam, *Treasures from the Misty Mountains: A Collector's Guide to Tolkien*. Burlington, Ontario: 2001. A very useful and entertaining compilation of Tolkien's books, including various editions, calendars, motion pictures, music inspired by Tolkien's works, and much more.

J.E.A. Tyler, *The New Tolkien Companion*. New York: St. Martin's Press, 1979. A very handy guide to Tolkien's writings. Not as comprehensive as Foster's book (see above), but still worthwhile.

Other Works Relating to *The Lord of the Rings* and J.R.R. Tolkien

Alida Becker, ed., *A Tolkien Treasury*. Philadelphia: Courage, 2000.

Norman F. Cantor, *Inventing the Middle Ages: The Lives, Works, and Ideas of Great Medievalists of the Twentieth Century*. New York: William Morrow, 1993.

Humphrey Carpenter, *The Inklings: C.S. Lewis, J.R.R. Tolkien, Charles Williams, and Their Friends*. London: Allen and Unwin, 1978.

Lin Carter, *Tolkien: A Look Behind* The Lord of the Rings. New York: Ballantine, 1969.

Jane Chance, *Tolkien's Art: A "Mythology for England."* New York: St. Martin's Press, 1979.

———, ed., *Tolkien the Medievalist*. London: Routledge, 2002.

Robley Evans, *J.R.R. Tolkien*. New York: Crowell, 1972.

Brandon Geist, ed., *The QPB Companion to* The Lord of the Rings. New York: Quality Paperback Book Club, 2001.

Daniel Grotta, *The Biography of J.R.R. Tolkien: Architect of Middle-Earth*. Philadelphia: Running Press, 1978.

Randel Helms, *Tolkien's World*. Boston: Houghton Mifflin, 1974.

Paul H. Kocher, *Master of Middle-Earth: The Fiction of J.R.R. Tolkien*. Boston: Houghton Mifflin, 1972.

Katie de Koster, ed., *Readings on J.R.R. Tolkien*. San Diego: Greenhaven Press, 2000.

Jared Lobdell, ed., *A Tolkien Compass*. La Salle, IL: Open Court, 1975.

Stephen O. Miller, *Middle-Earth: A World of Conflict*. Baltimore: T-K Graphics, 1975.

Joseph Pearce, *Tolkien: Man and Myth*. San Francisco: Ignatius, 1998.

Richard L. Purtill, *J.R.R. Tolkien: Myth, Morality, and Religion*. San Francisco: Harper and Row, 1984.

———, *Lord of the Elves and Eldils: Fantasy and Philosophy in C.S. Lewis and J.R.R. Tolkien*. Grand Rapids, MI: Zondervan, 1974.

Richard C. West, *Tolkien Criticism: An Annotated Checklist*. Kent, OH: Kent State University Press, 1981.

Index

allegory, 37
Aragorn (character), 47–49, 63
Auden, W.H., 12

Baggins, Bilbo (character)
  ballad of Earendil and, 44
  finding of the Ring and, 63
  friendship and, 62
  role of, in *Lord of the Rings* opening, 50
  role of, in *The Hobbit*, 52
Baggins, Frodo (character)
  description of, 49–50
  friendship and, 62
  heroism of, 60–61
  name origin of, 43
  ordinariness of, 60–61
  temptation and, 64
Beowulf (Old English epic), 42
Beowulf: The Monster and the Critics (Tolkien), 27
Bilbo. *See* Baggins, Bilbo
Boromir (character)
  description of, 47–49
  loyalty and, 63
  power and, 65–66
  temptation and, 64
Brandybuck, Merry (character), 51

Cantor, Norman F., 60, 61
characters, 47–58
  see also names of individual characters
Chaucer as a Philologist (Tolkien), 27
Christianity, 35, 63–64
Coren, Michael, 28
corruption, of power, 64–66
Crabbe, Katharyn, 39–40
Crist of Cynewulf (Old English poems), 44

dragons, 41, 43
dwarves, 41, 42–43, 52–53

Earendil (character), 44–45
Elder Edda (Norse myths), 41–42, 44
Elrond (character), 55, 66

Picture Credits

About the Author

Ted Hodges has been a fan and student of Tolkien's Ring trilogy for many years. This is his first book on the subject. Mr. Hodges lives in Minnesota with his wife, Mary.